THE HERMITAGE

THE HISTORY OF THE BUILDINGS AND COLLECTIONS

Alfa Colour
2009

Foreword by Mikhail Piotrovsky
Text by Vladimir Dobrovolsky
Translated from the Russian by Valery Fateyev
Design and layout by Alexander Rodionov
Photographs by Sergei Bogomiako, Vladimir Davydov, Pavel Demidov, Vladimir Denisov,
Leonard Kheifets, Yury Molodkovets, Yekaterina Poliak, Alexander Rodionov, Victor Savik,
Yevgeny Siniaver, Georgy Skachkov, Vladimir Terebenin and Valery Zubarov
Edited by Natalia Morozova
Computer layout by Meta Leif
Colour correction by Liubov Bogdanova,
Tatyana Chernyshenko and Inna Zezegova
Technical Director Peter Krakovsky

ISBN 978-5-9778-0051-8

THE HERMITAGE

THE HISTORY OF THE BUILDINGS AND COLLECTIONS

The Hermitage is a great museum that belongs both to Russia and the whole world. Millions of people come to St Petersburg to visit it, but it still retains the meaning of its name given by Catherine the Great, its founder. Even nowadays the Hermitage continues to be a "place of retreat". In all ages and under all regimes people have used to withdraw here from everyday concerns of the outside world.

The Hermitage has everything for that: the gold of the Scythians and ancient Greeks, Buddhist frescoes and Byzantine icons, Sassanian silver and Moslem bronzes; Chinese silks and Venetian lace, a brilliant collection of European paintings – Leonardo, Raphael, Titian, Rembrandt, Rubens, El Greco, Velázquez, Poussin, Cézanne, Matisse, Picasso, Kandinsky, Malevich, etc., jewellery by Pauzié and Fabergé, Sèvres and Wedgwood services, English silver and Augsburg gold tableware. It also owns a whole galaxy of magnificent architectural monuments that are noteworthy themselves as rare and edifying exhibits. The buildings of the Hermitage form a veritable museum of architectural landmarks. They also function as a prominent town-building complex – the heart of St Petersburg.

The Hermitage is a unique phenomenon of Russian culture and at the same time a monument to Russian statehood. Its buildings have witnessed many epoch-making events in Russian history. Among its inhabitants were not only Peter the Great, Catherine the Great and the other Emperors, but Prime Minister Stolypin, too. It was here that the mortally wounded Alexander II died, the inauguration of the First State Duma

1 **View of the Winter Palace from the Side of the Palace Embankment.**
1754–62. Architect: Bartolomeo Francesco Rastrelli

was celebrated and the Provisional Government having its session was arrested. And it was the Hermitage that became a symbol of the resistance of culture to the universal evil during the siege of Leningrad.

The life of the Hermitage Museum is an incessant movement of progress and change. Overcoming difficulties but invariably keeping its deeply rooted traditions, based on the traditions of Russian cultural policy, the Hermitage is known for its openness to the entire world. To those who are unable or have no time to visit the Hermitage, the museum tries to come itself – in the form of art books, TV films, Internet pages and temporary exhibitions. The display centres of the Hermitage function successfully in various cities of Russia and the world. The construction of the largest stock repository open for the general public is nearing completion.

The Hermitage is invariably glad to meet its numerous guests enjoying the museum's masterpieces and welcomes everybody who loves the beauty, labour and art of talented creative hands.

MIKHAIL PIOTROVSKY
Director of the State Hermitage,
Corresponding Member of the Russian Academy of Sciences,
Full Member of the Russian Academy of Arts,
Professor of St Petersburg University,
Doctor of Science (History)

THE HERMITAGE: THE HISTORY OF ITS DEVELOPMENT

Golitsyn, Catherine purchased excellent picture galleries set for sale by descendants of famous art collectors – of the Saxonian Minister Heinrich von Brühl (1769), the French Baron Pierre Crozat (1772), the English Lord Robert Walpole (1779), and her purchases shocked well-educated Europeans. In 1774 the Hermitage collection grew to more than 2,000 paintings and in 1796, the year of Catherine's demise, it numbered as many as four thousand pieces! Besides the paintings, the pride of the Hermitage became its huge collection of gemstones, a great number of medals and a luxurious library. The Empress was not very

The date of the establishment of the Hermitage Museum is taken to be the year 1764 when Catherine the Great became the owner of the first collection of 225 paintings by Western European masters received in payment for his debts from the Berlin merchant Johann Ernst Gotzkowsky who had amassed the collection for Frederick II of Prussia. The paintings brought to St Petersburg were intended for the Hermitage Pavilion then under construction. Such pavilions, fashionable in eighteenth-century France, were created, as their name suggested, for an isolated rest and intimate receptions.

Inspired by her successful acquisition, the Empress grew passionately infatuated with art collecting. Using the prompting of such qualified advisors as Denis Diderot, Melchior Grimm and Prince Dmitry

2 **Johann-Baptiste Lampi (1751–1830)** *Portrait of Catherine the Great.* **1793** Oil on canvas. 290 x 208 cm. Austria

3 **Franz von Krüger (1797–1857)** *Portrait of Nicholas I.* **1852** Oil on canvas. 93 x 73 cm. Germany

fond of sculpture. The superb collection of statuary of the English banker John Lyde Browne, acquired in 1787, was sent to Tsarskoye Selo and came to the Hermitage only in the nineteenth century.

A necessity to arrange all these treasures resulted in the construction, in the 1770s and 1780s, next to the Hermitage Pavilion (known as the Small Hermitage) of another building, the Large Hermitage, which formed, together with the theatre and the Raphael Loggias Block a whole complex of structures intended for private receptions.

Remaining the Empress's private property, the Hermitage became the most prominent feature of the capital and it could be visited for viewing with a special permission. Art lovers and foreign guests were amazed

4 **Permanent ticket for entrance to the Imperial Hermitage, the Gallery of Peter the Great and the Treasure Gallery for the year 1858**

5 **Konstantin Ukhtomsky.**
The Kolyvan Vase Hall
1858. Watercolour. 29.4 x 40 cm. Russia

by the "immense dimensions of its halls and galleries", so incongruous with its name, "by the wealth of its décor" and by paintings hanging "without order and selection". Professors and pupils of the Academy of Arts were allotted a special gallery for making copies. The first descriptions of the collections appeared in the reign of Catherine the Great.

In the first half of the nineteenth century a rapid growth of the collection of Classical Antiquity began, both thanks to new acquisitions and owing to sensational archaeological finds in the south of Russia. At the same time there appeared finds from the Ancient East, private memorial collections of Peter the Great were transferred from the Kunstkammer and the Treasure Gallery was established. A restoration school attached to the picture gallery was created. A thorough work on the inventory and study of the artifacts began. The arrival in the Hermitage of representatives of academic science made it an intellectual centre of the European level. The Hermitage's collection of

painting was markedly augmented with works of the Spanish school amassed by the English banker William Coesevelt (1814), a large part of the collection previously owned by Napoleon's consort Joséphine de Beauharnais (1815) and Italian paintings from the Venetian palace of the Barbarigo family (1850). These acquisitions enabled the Hermitage picture gallery to rank with the best art collections of the world. In 1824 a special department of Russian painting was formed (it existed until 1898).

In 1852 the construction of the New Hermitage building, put up by orders of Nicholas I, was finished. Despite constant reminding that the Hermitage belonged to the palace office, it began to acquire the significance of a state treasury. "Utter the word 'Hermitage'! At any corner of Russia – everyone heard about it," exclaimed the Russian writer Dmitry Grigorovich.

In 1864 the position of Director, responsible for the upkeep of the Hermitage and endowed with certain independence, was established. The first

director of the museum became Stepan Gedeonov, who did much to make the collections accessible.

In the second half of the nineteenth and the early twentieth centuries the museum acquired the first-rate collection of antiques of the Marquis Gian Pietro Campana (1861) and the famous collection of medieval art of Alexander Bazilewsky (1885). But large purchases of collections of paintings nearly ceased owing to a notable reduction of the museum's budget. The exclusion was an immense collection of Dutch and Flemish paintings bought in 1910 from the famous geographer Piotr Semionov-Tien-Shansky for the sum twice smaller than the owner had been offered in the West. The picture gallery augmented mainly thanks to individual purchases and bequests of collections to the Hermitage by their owners. Thus, in 1911–12 two priceless collections were added to the museum – that of English art previously owned by Alexei Khitrovo and of the Old Italian Masters accumulated by Sergei Stroganov. Remarkable events were

the Hermitage's acquisitions of *The Litta Madonna* by Leonardo da Vinci in 1865 and *The Benois Madonna* by the same great painter in 1914.

The great upheavals brought to the world by the twentieth century affected the Hermitage, too. At the outbreak of the First World War the museum's masterpieces were evacuated to Moscow and it took great efforts after the October Revolution to get them back. In the very difficult conditions of famine and devastation predominant in the early years of Soviet power the Hermitage, now a state

< 6 **Stepan Gedeonov (1815–1878).**
Lithographed photograph

< 7 **Iosif Orbeli (1887–1961).** Photograph

8 **Boris Piotrovsky (1908–1990).** Photograph

9 **Mikhail Piotrovsky.** Photograph

museum, became an abode for a whole stream of art values that flooded from nationalized palaces, churches and smaller museums and as a result the Hermitage collections grew fourfold. The temporal and geographical scope of the museum's collections greatly increased, which lent to the Hermitage the status of a museum of world culture.

There were losses, too. By orders of the country's authorities many Hermitage exhibits were taken out of their carefully chosen collections and transferred to other museums of the Soviet Union. In the 1920s a secret sale of Hermitage masterpieces abroad was undertaken. It was ceased largely owing to the courageous position of the museum staff and primarily of its future director, Iosif Orbeli. By that time, however, the Hermitage had lost the best paintings by Raphael, Titian, Velázquez, Rembrandt, Jan van Eyck, Botticelli and many other great artists.

Nevertheless the Hermitage Museum led an active life and developed – new departments were being formed, archaeological expeditions were arranged, scientific, exhibition and educational work was in full swing.

The War of 1941–45 turned out to be a severe trial for the Hermitage. Thanks to the foresight and daring of Academician Orbeli the museum proved to be ready for the war tribulations and the major part of the collections were happily evacuated behind the Urals. The remaining staff members in besieged Leningrad, despite unbearable difficulties, succeeded in preserving the museum that flung its doors open for visitors as early as November 1944.

The most recent major acquisition of the picture gallery was a transfer to the Hermitage in 1948 of 316 paintings by French masters of the turn of the nineteenth and twentieth centuries previously kept in the Museum of New Western Art, Moscow.

Admittedly, they were put on display for general visitors only ten years later.

A qualitatively new phase in the history of the museum started in the middle of the 1950s. Despite the "iron curtain" dividing the world into fighting camps, the Hermitage was accepted to the International Museum Council. Contacts with museums in diverse sections of the globe began to be maintained. The Hermitage became a centre of world tourism. An outstanding role in winning recognition by world society for the museum was played by its directors, Professor Mikhail Artamonov and especially Academician Boris Piotrovsky.

Today the State Hermitage is a great, dynamically developing centre of world science and culture. Its permanently growing collections number about 3,000,000 exhibits. The number of annual visitors to the Hermitage surpassed the border of three million people! The museum occupies nine buildings in St Petersburg alone and it has opened its branches in Kazan, London, Amsterdam and Las Vegas. The large-scale repository provided with up-to-date equipment that is being built for the stocks of the museums is to become a new cultural centre of the northern capital.

According to the concept of the museum developed and realized under the supervision of its present-day Director, Mikhail Piotrovsky, its basic strategic task for the new century is to attract to the special world named the Hermitage as much people as possible. The museum can attain this purpose only bringing together into an inseparable whole its exhibition, educational and entertainment activities.

10 > **The Winter Palace. Central section of the façade as viewed from Palace Square**

THE WINTER PALACE: A HISTORY

The Hermitage is famous not only for its collections, but for its buildings, too. The most remarkable place among them belongs to the Winter Palace that served as the principal residence of the Russian Emperors for 250 years. Together with the Admiralty, the General Staff and the Headquarters of the Guards Corps it forms a beautiful architectural complex of Palace Square that has become the architectural and historical centre of St Petersburg.

The first to choose the site for the construction of the Winter Palace in this place, at the beginning of the delta of the Neva, was Peter the Great. A magnificent panoramic view of the endless space of the smooth Neva with its islands, the reliable walls and guns of the Peter and Paul Fortress and the Admiralty – all was taken into consideration by the great founder of the city. Three Winter Palaces were successively built on the territory between the Neva, the Winter Canal and Millionnaya Street in Peter's lifetime. The last of them stood on the site of the present-day Hermitage Theatre. Peter the Great died in it in 1725.

From 1727, after the death of Peter's consort Empress Catherine I, the palace ceased to function as the royal residence. Peter II moved with his courtyard to Moscow where he soon died. On her return to St Petersburg in 1732, Empress Anna Ioannovna settled in the palace that had formerly belonged to Admiral Fiodor Apraxin. The building stood near the Admiralty and was the largest palatial structure in St Petersburg. But it did not satisfy the Empress who was fond of luxury, and the court architects – Carlo Francesco Rastrelli and his son Bartolomeo – began the work on the extension and inner reconstruction of the palace that lasted for decades.

With the elevation to the throne of Elizabeth Petrovna, the younger architect, Bartolomeo Francesco Rastrelli, was put in charge of the Winter Palace. In 1754 he offered to the Empress to demolish the old building and to put up on its site a new, immense edifice. According to the plan, the blocks of the palace skirted by an elaborately profiled fronts, two kilometers in length, were to form a rectangle with a large square in the centre. The nearly 25-metre height of the walls was to be used as a giant pedestal for

176 majestic statues of Olympic gods arranged on the roof. The lavish Baroque décor was to give to the edifice a sense of "eternal holiday", loved so much by the "merry Empress".

The project was based on four corner projections jutting out beyond the line of the front. It was planned to arrange within them the Main Staircase, the Throne Room, the Main Church and the Theatre (Opera House). The projections were to be linked by suites of rooms. The state rooms formed the Northern (Neva) and Eastern Enfilades. The Western Enfilade overlooking the Admiralty and the Southern Enfilade facing Palace Square were to be used as dwelling apartments.

The Empress accepted this daring plan. Asking the Senate to allot the sum of 900,000 roubles for the construction of the palace, Elizabeth declared that she was building it "for the glory of the Russian Empire alone". The large-scale construction work lasted for seven years. Nearly two and a half people were busy at the same time at masonry work, while the glazing of all the rooms and halls took 23,000 panes. "The overall

number of rooms in the palace is more than 460... all are decorated with the utmost magnificence," wrote Rastrelli. Empress Elizabeth did her best to accelerate the progress of work, but she died at the end of 1761 before the completion of the palace.

After a brief reign of Peter III the palace had a new owner – Empress Catherine II who had overthrown her consort. Catherine II (known as "Great") ruled the country for 34 years and all that time construction work in the Winter Palace and adjoining areas did not cease. Rastrelli's lavish Baroque splendour was not to Catherine's taste, so she dismissed the great architect replacing him by representatives of then fashionable Classicism. Starting from 1762, the

< 11 **Lucas Conrad Pfandzelt (1716–1788)** ***Portrait of Architect Bartolomeo Francesco Rastrelli.* 1750s–1760s.** Oil on canvas. Germany

< 12 **Unknown artist. *Fire in the Winter Palace in 1837. View from the Neva.* 1837.** Drawing

13 **Ferdinand Victor Perrot (1808–1841) *View of the Winter Palace from the South-Western Corner.* 1841** Lithograph. Watercolour. 45.0 x 57.2 cm. France

architects Jean-Baptiste Vallin de La Mothe, Yury Velten, Antonio Rinaldi, Ivan Starov and Giacomo Quarenghi worked on the creation of new halls and living apartments almost without interval. Soon only the Main Staircase and the Great Church remained from the interiors designed by Rastrelli.

The palace became the political and cultural centre of St Petersburg. Besides official receptions and ceremonies, its halls were used for balls and masquerades. Until the addition of the Small Hermitage the Empress's collection had been preserved in this building. Music could be heard in the Opera House.

After the first children had been born to the successor Grand Duke Pavel Petrovich, with their grandmother taking an active part in their education, the inner layout was changed and became close to what we see today. The Theatre was dismantled as a new building was put up for it. The Throne Room was shifted from the north-western projection into a special block linking the Winter Palace and the Small Hermitage. The enlarged dwelling section was divided into relatively isolated living apartments.

Considerable alterations were undertaken in the palace under Nicholas I, too. In the eastern block there appeared the War Gallery of 1812 and new state halls executed to projects by the architects Carlo Rossi and Auguste de Montferrand. A short time given to the builders and a wide use of wooden structures led to a tragedy. On 17 December 1837 a fire broke out in the imperial residence and as a result only charred walls remained from the beautiful building in 36 hours. The restoration of the palace was entrusted to the architects Vasily Stasov and Alexander Briullov, and under their supervision the Winter Palace was largely restored merely within 15 months.

With the passage of time candles began to be replaced with electric light, stoves and fireplaces were ousted by warm air heating and luxury gave way to cosiness. But the main thing remained unchanged – the palace was a home for the imperial family.

Everything, however, changed in February 1917 when the Winter Palace was turned into the residence of the Provisional Government. In October 1917 the Bolsheviks, who seized power, converted the palace into a museum of victorious revolution. In 1922 by a decree of the Soviet government the Winter Palace became the State Hermitage Museum.

14 **The Winter Palace. Central section of the façade as viewed from Palace Square. 1754 –62.**
Architect: Bartolomeo Francesco Rastrelli

15 > **The Winter Palace. Detail of the railing of the entrance gate. 1880s.**
Architect: Nikolai Gornostayev

19
**The Great Church
of the Winter Palace. View of
the dome from the south-east**

20
**View of the city from the roof
of the Winter Palace**

21 >
**View of the Cathedral
of the Resurrection
("The Savour-on-the-Spilt-Blood")
from the roof of the Winter Palace**

The State Halls of the Winter Palace

The construction and decoration of the state halls of the Winter Palace, personifying the might of the country, were entrusted to the foremost architects active in Russia. The restoration of the interiors destroyed by fire in 1837 was entrusted to the architect Vasily Stasov. Their décor is a mixture of styles of different ages – it reflects a desire of Emperor Nicholas I to restore everything "as it had been".

The "parade' section of the palace began from the Main or Jordan Staircase, which was used by foreign guests ascending to the palace as well as by the royal family going out to the "Jordan" (a hole cut in the ice on the Neva) during the celebration of the feast of Baptism. Stasov restored the staircase in the spirit of Rastrelli's Baroque. The immense space flooded with light, the dynamic outlines of the marble flights of stairs, the glistening gilding of ornaments, the majestic sculpture and the ceiling painting with Olympian gods, a work of the Italian painter Gasparo Diziani, all lends to the Jordan Staircase a mood of joyful exuberance restrained by the austere rhythm of grey granite columns. Two suites of state rooms – the Neva and Great Enfilades – diverge from the upper landing.

Re-created in the austere classical style characteristic of Quarenghi's interiors, the Neva Enfilade begins with the Anteroom. The next interior, covering an area of 1,103 metres, is the largest in the Winter Palace. After the death of Nicholas I a formal portrait of the Emperor painted by the German artist Franz von Krüger was put on display here. Since then the hall became known as the Nicholas Hall. The Neva Enfilade completes with the Concert Hall decorated with statues of the Muses. In 1922 the silver tomb of St Alexander Nevsky, created in St Petersburg in the middle of the eighteenth century, was transferred to the Concert Hall.

The halls of the Great Enfilade are united by the idea of the grandeur of the Russian Empire. The austere and majestic décor of the Field Marshals' Hall, called to celebrate the victories of the Russian arms, serves as an addition to the portraits of famous Russian military commanders of the eighteenth and nineteenth centuries.

The next interior after it, the memorial Peter Hall, symbolizes the unbreakable unity of the ruling dynasty. The central place here belongs to the portrait of Peter the Great painted by the Italian artist Jacopo Amiconi. The first Russian Emperor is depicted with the clever goddess of war Minerva. The walls of the hall are lined with velvet embroidered in silver with the state emblem of Russia and the monograms of Peter the Great.

The Peter Hall, small in area, contrasts with an immense Armorial Hall glistening with lavishly used gold. Its bronze chandeliers are adorned with shields bearing the coats-of-arms of the Russian provinces. The representations of the coats-of-arms earlier could also be seen on the spear shafts of the sculptural compositions arranged in the corners of the hall.

Parallel to the Armorial Hall runs the famous War Gallery devoted to the victory of the Russian troops

21

in the Patriotic War of 1812. On its walls are arranged portraits of 332 generals, participants in the battles against the French troops. The portraits were painted by the English artist George Dawe assisted by the Russian painters Vasily Golicke and Alexander Poliakov. The mounted formal portrait of Emperor Alexander I was executed by Franz von Krüger.

The Great Enfilade completes with the Throne Room or St George Hall. The noble combination of snow-white Carrara marble and ormolu endows the principal hall of the palace with a special spirit of majesty. The throne, bound with silver-gilt, was produced as early as 1731 by the English master craftsman Nicholas Clausen for Empress Anna Ioannovna. Over the throne place, re-created in 2000, hangs a marble relief depicting St George, the patron of Russia, a work by Franco del Nero.

Next to the Great Enfilade is the cathedral that had formerly been consecrated to the Vernicle (a sacred image of the Saviour). Restoring the cathedral after the fire, Stasov did his best to retain its original Baroque décor created by Rastrelli. The architectural shapes filled with powerful movement, the glistening of gold and painted decoration, all here blends into a single accord glorifying the Almighty.

The only state hall overlooking Palace Square is the Alexander Hall. Designed by Alexander Briullov, it is devoted to Emperor Alexander I and to Russia's victory over France and is a vivid example of a happy combination of diverse architectural styles. Its walls are embellished with moulded allegorical compositions illustrating the war against Napoleon Bonaparte. The depictions are based on a series of memorial medals created by the sculptor Fiodor Tolstoy.

25
**The Main (Jordan) Staircase.
Detail of the decoration**

26 >
The Main (Jordan) Staircase. 1754–62; 1838–39. Detail
Architects: Bartolomeo Francesco Rastrelli; Vasily Stasov

27 **Eduard Hau (1816–1895)**
The Great Field Marshals' Hall. **1866**
Watercolour. 33.1 x 42.6 cm. Russia

28 **The Field Marshals' Hall.**
1833; 1838–39. Architects:
Auguste de Montferrand; Vasily Stasov

29 > **Nicolas Sébastien Froste**
(1790–1856). *Portrait of Generalissimo*
Count Alexander Suvorov. **1834**
Oil on canvas. 360 x 219 cm. France

30 > **Franz von Krüger (1797–1857)**
Portrait of General Field
Marshal Prince Ivan Paskevich. **1834**
Oil on canvas. 360 x 219 cm. Germany

31 > **Piotr Basin (1793–1877)**
Portrait of General Field Marshal
Prince Mikhail Kutuzov. **1833–34**
Oil on canvas. 360 x 219 cm. Russia

< 32
The Peter Hall (Small Throne Room).
1833; 1838−39 Architects:
Auguste de Montferrand; Vasily Stasov

33
The Peter Hall (Small Throne Room).
Ceiling painting

34
The Peter Hall (Small Throne Room).
Detail of the niche with the imperial crown
and the monogram of Peter the Great

35 >>
The Armorial Hall. 1838−39
Architect: Vasily Stasov

< 36
The Armorial Hall. Sculptural group: knights with banners and standards. 1839
Sculptor: Julius Streichenberg.
Russia

37
**The Armorial Hall.
Gilded capitals of the columns**
Detail

38
Adolph Ladurner (1798–1856)
View of the White (Armorial) Hall in the Winter Palace. **1838**
Oil on canvas. 69 x 96 cm. Russia

39
Franz von Krüger (1797–1857). *Equestrian Portrait of*
Emperor Alexander I. **1837.** Oil on canvas. 484 x 344 cm. Germany

40 >
The War Gallery of 1812. 1826; 1838–39
Architects: Carlo Rossi; Vasily Stasov

< 41
George Dawe (1781–1829)
Portrait of Piotr Bagration.
Ca **1823.** Oil on canvas.
70 x 62.5 cm. England

< 42
George Dawe (1781–1829)
Portrait of Alexander Tuchkov.
Ca **1825.** Oil on canvas.
70 x 62.5 cm. England

< 43
George Dawe (1781–1829)
Portrait of Nikolai Rayevsky.
Ca **1828.** Oil on canvas.
70 x 62.5 cm. England

< 44
George Dawe (1781–1829)
Portrait of Denis Davydov.
Ca **1828.** Oil on canvas.
70 x 62.5 cm. England

45
George Dawe (1781–1829)
Portrait of General
Field Marshal
Prince Mikhail Kutuzov.
1829. Oil on canvas.
361 x 268 cm. England

< 46 **The Large Throne Room (St George Hall).**
1838–41. Architect: Vasily Stasov

47 **The Large Throne Room (St George Hall).**
Throne. Made by Nicholas Clausen.
1731. Silver-gilt. England

< 48 The Great Church of the Winter Palace. 1754–62; 1838–39.
Architects: Bartolomeo Francesco Rastrelli; Vasily Stasov

49 The Great Church of the Winter Palace.
Shield with the monogram of Empress
Elizabeth Petrovna. Detail of the decoration

50 The Great Church of the Winter Palace.
The Evangelist Matthew and the Angel
Artist: Fiodor Bruni. Pendentive of the dome

51 Loritz Regner Tuxen (1853–1927). *The Wedding of*
Emperor Nicholas II and Empress Alexandra Fiodorovna.
1895. Oil on canvas. 65.6 x 87.5 cm. Denmark

< 52 **The Alexander Hall.**
Details of the architectural décor: moulded trophy

< 53 **The Alexander Hall.**
Details of the architectural décor:
moulded mask shaped like a lion's head

< 54 **Eduard Hau (1816–1895).**
The Alexander Hall. **1861**
Watercolour. 34.8 x 37.5 cm. Russia

55 **The Alexander Hall. 1838–39.**
Architect: Alexander Briullov

< 56
Tomb of St Alexander Nevsky.
1747–52 From a drawing by
Georg Christoph Grooth. Silver. Russia

57
The Concert Hall.
1791–93; 1830; 1838–39
Architects: Giacomo Quarenghi;
Auguste de Montferrand; Vasily Stasov.

58
Tomb of St Alexander Nevsky.
The regalia. Detail

The Dwelling Apartments of the Winter Palace

Unlike the décor of the state halls altered relatively rarely, the inner appearance of the dwelling apartments, designed according to the fashion of the period and tastes of their inhabitants, were changed fairly often. Many famous architects participated in the creation of these small interiors. History has retained to us the names of these rooms: the Brilliant Room of Catherine the Great, the Crystal Bedroom of Elizabeth Alexeyevna, the Pompeian Dining Room of Nicholas I... In the middle of the nineteenth century the artists Grigory and Nikanor Chernetsov, Konstantin Ukhtomsky, Eduard Hau and Luigi Premazzi created a series of watercolours with views of the rooms and halls of the Winter Palace and the Hermitage, recording their appearance for the memory of generations to come.

At the present time the Winter Palace has preserved only some of the superb dwelling apartments, which had once occupied a considerable place in the huge building.

The most famous among them is the Malachite Drawing Room designed by Alexander Briullov, who restored the dwelling apartments of the imperial residence after the fire of 1837. This room is a veritable gem in the apartments of Empress Alexandra Fiodorovna, Nicholas I's consort. The combination of golden, green, white and crimson colours make it one of the most orate interiors in the palace. The decoration of this state room executed in the Russian mosaic technique took more than two tonnes of malachite brought from the Urals.

In 1841, in connection with the wedding of Heir Tsesarevich Alexander Nikolayevich (the future Emperor Alexander II) and Maria Alexandrovna, Alexander Briullov created for the newlyweds the Heir's New Apartments, which later became the apartments of the Empress. From the interiors created by this architect survive the White Hall sustained in classical traditions and amply embellished with sculpture as well as the Gold Room amazing visitors by the abundance of gold and reminiscent in some way of the ancient chambers of the Moscow Kremlin. Later, in the 1850 and 1860s, the court architect Andrei Stackenschneider created in the apartments of Maria Alexandrovna a cosy Crimson Study that also served as the Empress's musical salon and the exquisite Green Dining Room. The fantasy of the architect Harald Bosse reveals itself in the sumptuous Boudoir, the decoration of which made in the Second Rococo style is reflected in numerous mirrors.

The last alterations in the dwelling apartments date from the reign of Nicholas II. Almost unaltered are the surviving Library and the Small Dining Room designed at the end of the nineteenth century to a project by the architect Alexander Krasovsky. The interior of the Library, treated in the Gothic style, evokes a feeling of calm and comfort disposing one

< 59 **Luigi Premazzi (1814–1891).**
The White Hall. **1865.** Watercolour. 40.8 x 33 cm. Italy

60 **The White Hall**
Architect: Alexander Briullov. 1838–41

to philosophical meditations. Decorated with medieval ornaments, the wooden panels, the stamped and gilded leather and the massive fireplace well combine with the carefully thought-out library equipment.

The decoration of the Small Dining Room intended for everyday meals is distinguished by lightness of moulded ornaments, while the glazed cupboards with crockery and the tapestries produced in St Petersburg in the eighteenth century, lend a special air of cosiness to this interior. The Small Dining Room is notable in Russian history as the place where the Provisional Government was arrested in October 1917, after the storm of the Winter Palace by the Bolsheviks.

< 61
The Gold Drawing Room. 1838–41; 1850s; late 1860s
Architects: Alexander Briullov;
Andrei Stackenschneider; Victor Schreiber

62
The Gold Drawing Room. Detail of the decoration of the ceiling painting. Shield with the monogram of Grand Duke Alexander Pavlovich (the future Emperor Alexander II)

63
**The Gold Drawing Room.
Detail of a standard lamp**
Second half of the 19th century.
Porcelain, gilded bronze. Russia

64
Eduard Hau (1816–1895)
The Boudoir of Empress Maria Alexandrovna.
1861 Watercolour. 27 x 27.4 cm. Russia

65
The Boudoir. Marble caryatid
Detail of the architectural décor

The Boudoir. 1853. Architect: Harald Bosse

< 67
**The Crimson
Drawing Room (Study).
1838–41; 1850s**
Architects: Alexander Briullov;
Andrei Stackenschneider

68
**The Crimson Drawing Room
(Study). Shield with the monogram
of Empress Maria Alexandrovna**
Detail of the architectural décor

69
Luigi Premazzi (1814–1891)
*The Study of Empress
Maria Alexandrovna.* **1869**
Watercolour. 35 x 45.4 cm. Italy

70
Luigi Premazzi (1814–1891)
The Green Dining Room. **1852**
Watercolour. 27 x 34.4 cm. Italy

71 >
The Green Dining Room. 1850
Architect: Andrei Stackenschneider

72 >>
The Malachite Drawing Room. 1838–39
Architect: Alexander Briullov

< 73
The Malachite Drawing Room
Detail of the interior

74
Konstantin Ukhtomsky (1818–1881)
The Malachite Drawing Room. **1865**
Watercolour. 27.8 x 39 cm. Russia

75
The Malachite Drawing Room.
Showcase with table decorations
19th century. Russia

76 **Eduard Hau (1816–1895)**
The Third Hall of Battle Paintings. **1866**
Watercolour. 31.6 x 45 cm. Russia

77 > **The Hall of French 18th-Century Art. 1838–39**
Architect: Alexander Briullov

78 > **Etienne Maurice Falconet (1716–1791)**
Menacing Cupid. **1766–67**
Marble. Height 85 cm. France

< 79
The Library of Nicholas I. 1894–96. Architect: Alexander Krasovsky

80
The Small Dining Room. 1894–96. Architect: Alexander Krasovsky

81
The Small Dining Room. Mantel clock. Mid-18th century. France

82 The display of the Department
of Archaeology of Eastern Europe
and Siberia (the former Drawing
Room with Cupids)
Detail of the architectural décor

83 Eduard Hau (1816–1895)
The Drawing Room in the Second
Rococo Style (with Cupids). **1860s**
Watercolour. 25.7 x 32 cm. Russia

84 > The display of the Department
of Archaeology of Eastern Europe
and Siberia (the former Drawing
Room with Cupids). **1856**
Architect: Andrei Stackenschneider

FRANCE: 15TH TO 20TH CENTURY

The Hermitage collection of French art is thought to be the best outside France. It reflects the immense influence exerted by France – the model of European taste and luxury – on Russia. The exhibition of French art in the Winter Palace occupies more than sixty halls and contains numerous works of painting, sculpture and decorative art from the late fifteenth to twentieth century. The nucleus of the Hermitage collection took shape in the eighteenth century under Catherine the Great. After the revolution of 1917 new acquisitions of Western art to the Hermitage practically ceased. It was only in 1922 that the museum was enriched with the collection of paintings previously owned by Alexander Kushelev-Bezborodko, who collected French painting of the first half of the nineteenth century – works by the Romanticists and landscapes of the Barbizon school. The paintings dating to the late nineteenth and early twentieth centuries from the former collection of Sergei Shchukin and Ivan Morozov arrived at the Hermitage from Moscow in 1948. In the recent years the State Hermitage began to acquire works of French artists at international auctions.

French art of the fifteenth and sixteenth centuries is basically represented in the museum by works of decorative and applied art: Limoges enamels, faience, furniture and tapestries, with some rare examples of painting and sculpture. These works, created under the influence of Italian art, already betray that "clever calculation and subtle feeling of measure" which would become characteristic of French art in the subsequent periods.

In the conditions of royal absolutism the leading role in seventeenth-century French art came to belong to Classicism "preoccupied with the contemplation of eternal truths". The Hermitage owns paintings by outstanding adherents of Classicism – the lofty dreamer Nicolas Poussin, the creator of ideal nature Claude Lorraine and the "painter of reality" Louis Le Nain, whose works are pervaded with an epic calm.

In the eighteenth century the French artistic genius created the magic world of the Rococo – a light, playful, erotic style that reigned in all aristocratic salons and boudoirs. A kind of a Rococo symbol in the Hermitage may be regarded the charming marble *Cupid* by Etienne Maurice Falconet. The founder of the Rococo Antoine Watteau, a great artist, painted touching pictures known as *scènes galantes*, in which the mood of joyful carelessness neighbours with the sense of tiredness, indifference and solitude. Works by his pupils and followers – the virtuoso Nicolas Lancret or François Boucher, Marquise de Pompadour's favourite artist, or the warm and joyous Jean Honoré Fragonard reflect, on the contrary, only the outward, festive side of life.

In French art of the second half of the eighteenth century there appeared trends meeting the demands and tastes of the third estate. The most vivid exponent of these changes was Jean-Baptiste Chardin, who managed to show in his paintings the beauty of everyday life of common people and of the objects surrounding them. The edifying scenes by Jean-Baptiste Greuze and Realist sculptural portraits by Jean Antoine Houdon represent French art of the Enlightenment period.

< 85
Bernard Palissy (1510–1589). *Dish. Ca 1560.*
Faience. 47.5 x 35 cm. France

86
The Adoration of the Magi. **Central part of a triptych.**
Early 16th century Copper, painted in enamels.
28x 38.8 cm. Haut Face workshop, Limoges

87 **Plate with a depiction of Psyche feasting her
eyes upon the sleeping Cupid. Mid-16th century.**
Copper, painted in enamels. Diameter 23.5 cm.
Workshop of Pierre Reymond, Limoges

88 **Master of the Thuison Altarpiece.**
*The Entry of Christ into Jerusalem
(wing of an altarpiece).* Second half of the
15th century, Oil on panel. 116.5 x 51.5 cm. France

The upheavals of the turn of the eighteenth and nineteenth centuries, connected with the Great French Revolution and Napoleon's ascend to power, brought back an interest in Classicism, the foremost exponents of which were Jacques Louis David and his pupils Antoine Jean Gros and Jacques Auguste Dominique Ingres. At the same time a new Romantic movement based on a direct impression of concrete events was taking a firm root. Eugène Delacroix, the most prominent Romantic artist, in search for a source of inspiration travelled to exotic countries and then literally fired the viewer's imagination by his powerful painting.

The canvases by the Barbizon painters, the founders of national landscape painting Théodore Rousseau, Jules Dupret, Constant Troyon, Charles Daubigny and Camille Corot, who was close to them, plunge lovers of painting into the lyrical and romantic realm of rural France.

A place apart in the artistic life of nineteenth-century France belonged to the Paris Salons – exhibitions of the artists whose works were admitted by the Academic jury. The main demands to the paintings were to be accessible to understanding, technically perfect and entertaining in subject-matter. A challenge to Salon art became works by the Impressionists Claude Monet, Pierre Auguste Renoir, Camille Pissarro and Alfred Sisley, who sought to capture fleeting impressions in their strikingly colourful pictures. The great Auguste Rodin tried to solve a similar task in sculpture. The mighty willpower and intellect of Paul Cézanne, the impulsive intensity of Vincent van Gogh and the pacifying contemplation of Paul Gauguin, all these qualities found reflection in the distinctive artistic idiom of these painters.

A sincere spontaneity and artistic ingenuity became the principal criteria in twentieth-century art, represented in the Hermitage by numerous works of well-known masters, including the world-famous decorative canvases by Henri Matisse and Pablo Picasso.

89
**Claude Gellée,
called Lorrain (1600–1682)**
Morning in a Harbour. **1640s**
Oil on canvas. 74 x 97 cm. France

90 >
Simon Vouet (1590–1649)
Allegorical Portrait of Anne of Austria. Ca **1643**
Oil on canvas. 202 x 172 cm. France

67

91
Pierre Dumoustier the Elder
(*ca 1545 – before 1610*)
Portrait of a Youth.
Last decades of the 16th century.
Oil on canvas. 32 x 19 cm. France

92
Louis Le Nain (1593–1648).
The Milkmaid's Family. **1640s**
Oil on canvas. 51 x 59 cm. France

93
Corneille de Lyon
(**early 16th century – 1575**)
Female Portrait. **Mid-1530s**
Oil on panel. 20 x 15.5 cm. France

94
Nicolas Poussin (1594–1665)
Landscape with Polyphemus.
1649. Oil on canvas.
150 x 199 cm. France

95
Nicolas Poussin (1594–1665)
Tancred and Erminia.
1630–31. Oil on canvas.
98.5 x 146.5 cm. France

96
Antoine Watteau (1684–21) *Embarrassing Proposal.*
Ca **1716.** Oil on canvas. 65 x 84.5 cm. France

97
Antoine Watteau (1684–21) *Capricious Woman.*
Ca **1718.** Oil on canvas. 42 x 34 cm. France

98 >
Antoine Watteau (1684–21) *Actors of the Thêâtre Française.*
Ca **1712.** Oil on panel. 20 x 25 cm. France

99 >
Antoine Watteau (1684–21) *Savoyard with a Marmot*
Ca **1716.** Oil on canvas. 40.5 x 32.5 cm. France

100 >
Nicolas Lancret (1690–43) *Portrait of the Dancer La Camargo.*
1730s. Oil on canvas. 45 x 55 cm. France

101 **François Boucher (1703–70).** *Pastoral Scene.*
1740s. Oil on canvas. 61 x 75 cm. France

102 **François Boucher (1703–70)** *Landscape in the*
Environs of Beauvais. **Early 1740s**
Oil on canvas. 49 x 58 cm. France

103 > **Jean-Baptiste Siméon Chardin (1699–79)**
Still Life with the Attributes of the Arts. **1766**
Oil on canvas. 112 x 140.5 cm. France

104 > **Jean-Baptiste Perronneau (1715–83)**
Portrait of a Boy with a Book. **Mid-1740s**
Oil on canvas. 63 x 52 cm. France

105 > **Jean-Baptiste Siméon Chardin (1699–1779)**
A Washerwoman. **1730s.** Oil on canvas. 37.5 x 42.7 cm. France

106
Jean Honoré Fragonard (1732–1806)
A Stolen Kiss. **Late 1780s**
Oil on canvas. 45 x 55 cm. France

107
Jean-Baptiste Greuze (1725–1805)
The Paralytic or the Fruit of Good Education.
1763. Oil on canvas. 115.5 x 146 cm. France

108 >
Jean-Baptiste Greuze (1725–1805)
A Spoiled Child. **Early 1760s**
Oil on canvas. 66.5 x 56 cm. France

109 **Etienne Maurice Falconet (1716–1791).** *Winter.*
1771. Marble. Height 135 cm. France

110 *Pygmalion and Galatea.* **1766–73**
Biscuit. Height 36.5 cm. From a model
by Etienne Maurice Falconet. Sèvres, France

111 **Etienne Maurice Falconet (1716–1791)**
Menacing Cupid. **1766–67.** Marble. Height 85 cm. France

112 > **Jean Antoine Houdon (1741–1828)**
Voltaire Seated in an Armchair. **1781**
Marble. Height 138 cm. France

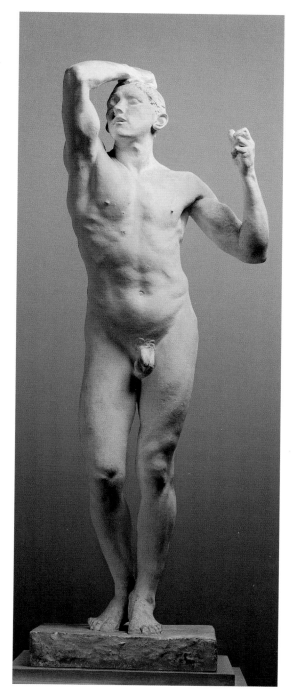

< 113
Auguste Rodin (1840–1917). *Eternal Spring.*
After 1884 Marble. Height 77 cm. France

114
Auguste Rodin (1840–1917). *Romeo and Juliet.* **1905**
Marble. Height 71 cm. France

115
Auguste Rodin (1840–1917). *The Bronze Age.* **1877**
Plaster of Paris. Height 175 cm

< 116
Antoine Jean Gros (1771–1835)
*Napoleon Bonaparte on the
Bridge at Arcole.* **1797.** Oil on canvas.
134 x 104 cm. France

117
Jacques Louis David (1748–1825)
Sappho and Phaon. **1809**
Oil on canvas. 225.3 x 262 cm. France

118
François Gérard (1770–1837)
Portrait of Joséphine. **1801**
Oil on canvas. 178 x 174 cm. France

119
**Léon Joseph
Florentin Bonnat
(1833–1922)**
In the Mountains
After 1870
Oil on canvas.
78.5 x 121.5 cm. France

120
**Eugène Delacroix
(1798–1863)**
Lion Hunt in Morocco
1854. Oil on canvas.
74 x 92 cm. France

121 >
**Eugène Delacroix
(1798–1863).**
*A Moroccan Saddling
His Horse.* **1855**
Oil on canvas.
56 x 47 cm. France

122
Emile Auguste Carolus-Durant (1837–1917)
Portrait of Nadezhda Polovtsova. **1876**
Oil on canvas. 206.5 x 124.5 cm. France

123
Camille Joseph Etienne Roqueplan (1803–1855)
Girl with Flowers. **1843.** Oil on canvas. 110 x 84 cm. France

124
François Xavier Winterhalter (1806–1873)
Portrait of Countess Sophia Naryshkina. **1858**
Oil on canvas. 150 x 114 cm. France

125 >
Jean Auguste Dominique Ingres (1780–1867)
Portrait of Nikolai Guryev. **1821**
Oil on canvas. 107 x 86 cm. France

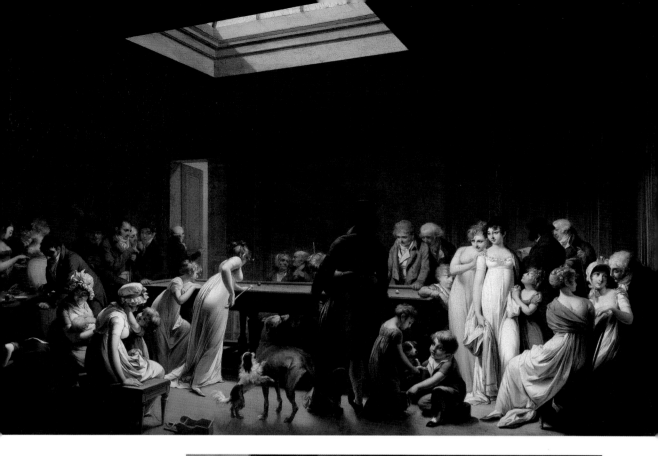

< 126
**Jean Léon Gérôme
(1824–1904)**
Sale of a Slave. Ca **1884**
Oil on canvas.
92 x 74 cm. France

127
**Louis Léopold Boilly
(1761–1845).**
Billiards. **1807**
Oil on canvas.
56 x 81 cm. France

128
Jules Lefèvre (1836–1912)
*Mary Magdalene in a
Grotto.* **1876.** Oil on canvas.
71.5 x 113.5 cm. France

129
**Jean-Baptiste Camille Corot
(1796–1875)**
Trees in a Marsh
Between 1855 and 1860
Oil on canvas.
25.5 x 38 cm. France

130
**Théodore Rousseau
(1812–1867)**
Market in Normandy. **1832 (?)**
Oil on panel. 29.5 x 38 cm. France

131 >
Constant Troyon (1810–1865)
Setting Out to Market. **1859**
Oil on canvas.
260.5 x 211 cm. France

132
Claude Oscar Monet (1840–1926)
Haystack at Giverny. **1886**
Oil on canvas. 61 x 81 cm. France

133
Claude Oscar Monet (1840–1926)
Lady in the Garden (Sainte-Addresse).
1867. Oil on canvas. 80 x 99 cm. France

134
Pierre Auguste Renoir (1841–1919).
Child with a Whip. **1885**
Oil on canvas. 105 x 75 cm. France

135
Pierre Auguste Renoir (1841–1919)
Portrait of the Actress Jeanne Samary. **1878**
Oil on canvas. 174 x 101.5 cm. France

136
Pierre Auguste Renoir (1841–1919)
Girl with a Fan. **1881.** Oil on canvas. 65 x 50 cm. France

137
Alfred Sisley (1839–1999)
Villeneuve la Garenne on the Seine. **1872**
Oil on canvas. 59 x 80.5 cm. France

138
Edgar Degas (1834–1917). *Woman Combing Her Hair*
(Woman at Her Toilet). **1885–86**
Pastel on cardboard. 53 x 52 cm. France

139 >
Camille Pissarro (1830–1903)
Boulevard Montmartre in Paris. **1897**
Oil on canvas. 73 x 92 cm. France

140 >
Armand Baptiste Guillaumin (1841–1927)
The Seine. **1867–69.** Oil on canvas. 26 x 50 cm. France

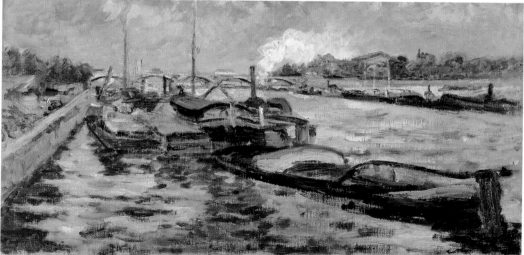

141
Paul Cézanne (1839–1906)
Still Life with Drapery. Ca **1899**
Oil on canvas. 55 x 74.5 cm. France

142
Vincent van Gogh (1853–1890)
***Cottages.* 1890.** Oil on canvas.
60 x 73 cm. France

143
Vincent van Gogh (1853–1890)
Lilac Bush. **1889.** Oil on canvas.
72 x 92 cm. France

144
Vincent van Gogh (1853–1890)
The Ladies of Arles
(Remembrance of the Garden at Etten)
1888. Oil on canvas. 73 x 92 cm. France

145
Paul Gauguin (1848–1903)
Tabitian Pastorals. **1893**
Oil on canvas. 87.5 x 113.7 cm. France

146
Paul Gauguin (1848–1903). *Sunflowers.*
1901. Oil on canvas. 73 x 92 cm. France

147 >
Paul Gauguin (1848–1903)
Woman Holding a Fruit. **1893**
Oil on canvas. 92 x 73 cm. France

148
Henri Matisse (1869–1954). *Vessels and Fruit*
1901. Oil on canvas. 51 x 61.5 cm. France

149
Henri Matisse (1869–1954). *Conversation*
1909. Oil on canvas. 177 x 217 cm. France

150
Henri Matisse (1869–1954)
The Dance. **1910**
Oil on canvas.
270 x 391 cm. France

151
Henri Matisse (1869–1954)
The Red Room
(Dessert. Harmony in Red).
1908. Oil on canvas.
180 x 220 cm. France

152
Pablo Picasso (1881–1973)
Tavern. Ca 1914. Oil on canvas.
29.5 x 38.7 cm. France

153
Pablo Picasso (1881–1973)
Lady with a Fan (After the Ball)
1908. Oil on canvas.
152 x 101 cm. France

154
Pablo Picasso (1881–1973)
The Absinthe Drinker. **1901.**
Oil on canvas. 73 x 54 cm. France

155 >
Pablo Picasso (1881–1973)
Guitar and Violin. **1912–13**
Oil on canvas. 65.5 x 54.3 cm. France

England: 16th to 19th Century

The collection of English art of the sixteenth to nineteenth century, represented by painting, sculpture and objects of decorative art, occupy four rooms in the Winter Palace. The collecting was started in the last decades of the eighteenth century, in connection with the activity of Catherine the Great and with the emergence of an unusual interest in English art in Russia during that period. Active in Russia in the nineteenth century were the English painters George Dawe, who created a series of portraits for the famous War Gallery, and the fashionable artist Christina Robertson. In 1912, according to the will of the well-known Anglomaniac Alexei Khitrovo, his large collection of English painting entered the Hermitage. Some of the exhibits were transferred to the museum in the 1920s from nationalized palaces.

Despite the general flowering of culture in England during the Renaissance, foreign masters dominated English fine art in the sixteenth and the first half of the seventeenth century. Among the artists active in Britain in the sixteenth century was the famous German portrait painter Hans Holbein the Younger.

Portraiture occupies a special place in the life of English people carefully preserving the memory of their ancestors. The English portraits of the sixteenth century are restrained, austere and devoid of any hint at expression.

In the seventeenth century the great Flemish painter Anthonis van Dyck laid the foundations of the national school of painting in England and created the new type of formal portraiture investing it, in addition to the feeling of dignity, with poetry and high spirituality. In the age of Enlightenment the excellent English painter Godfrey Kneller created in his works the image of free and proud creator and thinker. English art saw a flowering in the eighteenth century when great names began to appear in painting.

The most notable among them was William Hogarth, a graphic artist and a theoretician of art, but the Hermitage unfortunately does not possess his paintings. The subtlest lyrical artist Thomas Gainsborough, who created despite all rules and nevertheless attained amazing results, is represented in the Hermitage by one of his best works – *Portrait of a Lady in Blue*.

Joshua Reynolds managed to continue in England, to use the words of Eugène Delacroix, the "traditions of the greatest artists". The Hermitage owns three paintings by Reynolds and, notably, Catherine the Great herself commissioned one of them, *The Infant Hercules Strangling the Serpents*, from the master. The major nineteenth-century English portraitist Thomas Lawrence, never lowering himself to flattery, could emphasize the best features of his sitter and to meet the tastes of his

< 156 **Godfrey Kneller (1646/49?–1723).**
Portrait of Grinling Gibbons
Not later than 1690. Oil on canvas. 125 x 90 cm. England

157 **Thomas Gainsborough (1727–1788).**
Portrait of a Lady in Blue. **Late 1770s.**
Oil on canvas. 76 x 64 cm. England

high-ranking clientele, and Russian aristocrats among them.

For Englishmen, true lovers and connoisseurs of nature, creators of famous parks and gardens, landscape painting became the truly national kind of art that exerted an influence upon entire European painting. The Romantic canvases by Richard Parkes Bonington undoubtedly rank with the best landscape paintings in the Hermitage collection.

The superb collection of English silver of the seventeenth to nineteenth century numbers more than 200 exhibits. Its larger and better part dates from the eighteenth century and includes festive services, table decorations and toilet sets. Highly impressive are the luxurious vessels intended for wine-cooling. The largest of them, weighing more than 200 kilo-grammes and richly adorned with reliefs and sculptural details, was manufactured of silver by Charles Candler in 1734. The immense vessel was brought to Russia several years later. The pride of place in the collection of English pottery be-

longs to the pieces produced at the famous factory of Josiah Wedgwood and primarily to the faience Green Frog Service, commissioned by Catherine the Great. This service, comprising 944 items decorated with 1222 views of England, was intended for the suburban Chesme Palace.

The passion of Catherine the Great for carved gems is generally known and the Empress herself named it a "cameo disease". Besides acquisitions of already formed collections, of which that of the Duke of Orleans was the most significant, Catherine the Great also made commissions from contemporary English stone carvers, especially the best of them, the brothers Charles and William Brown, who made for her more than 200 gems.

< 158
**Marcus Geeraerts the Younger
(1561/62–1635/36).**
Portrait of an Unknown Man. **1595**
Oil on panel. 114.5 x 89 cm. England

< 159
**Richard Parkes Bonington
(1802–1828)**
Boats near the Shores of Normandy
Oil on canvas. 33.5 x 46 cm. England

160
George Morland (1763–1804)
Approaching Thunderstorm. **1791**
Oil on canvas. 85 x 117 cm. England

< 161
Joshua Reynolds (1723–1792)
Cupid Untying the Girdle of Venus. **1788**
Oil on canvas. 127.5 x 101 cm. England

162
Joshua Reynolds (1723–1792)
The Infant Hercules Strangling the Serpents.
1786–88. Oil on canvas. 303 x 297 cm. England

163
Christina Robertson (1775–1856)
Children with a Parrot. **1850s**
Oil on canvas. 112 x 104 cm. England

164 >
Thomas Lawrence (1769–1830)
Portrait of Count Mikhail Vorontsov. **1821**
Oil on canvas. 143 x 113 cm. England

165 Josiah Wedgwood (1730–1795).
Round dish: *View of the Despencer Family House*
in West Wycombe Park, Buckinghamshire
Etruria Factory. Diameter 24.5 cm

166 Josiah Wedgwood (1730–1795).
Items from the *Green Frog service.* 1773–74
Creamware, painted in colours over a glaze.
Etruria Factory. England

167 > William Brown (1748–25).
Intaglio: *The Head of Hygeia. Ca* 1785
Cornelian, golden mount. 3.0 x 2.7 cm. England

168 > Paul Crespin (1694–1770).
Two-handled goblet and cover. 1726–27
Silver-gilt. Height 34 cm. England

169 > Charles (Karl) Kändler
(active 1720s–1770s). Wine-cooler. 1734–35.
Silver. 100 x 169 x 98 cm. England

Germany: 15th to 20th Century

The art of Germany represented in the ten rooms of the Winter Palace covers a 500-year period from the late fifteenth to the middle of the twentieth century. The collection of German art, despite its considerable number, is not remarkable for its integrity and wholeness. It is due to the fact that European collectors lacked interest in painting by old German masters for a long time. Only two names – Albrecht Dürer and Hans Holbein the Younger, whose work is represented in the Hermitage by engravings, enjoyed a deserved fame.

The core of the collection of painting, formed under Catherine the Great, are works by German artists of the second half of the eighteenth century, which were actively purchased by the court and Russian aristocrats. The collection considerably grew in the reign of Nicholas I, largely thanks to the poet Vasily Zhukovsky who had an influence upon the Emperor. The canvases

by German painters of the second half of the nineteenth and early twentieth centuries came to the Hermitage from private collections nationalized after the revolution.

German art of the fifteenth and sixteenth centuries, represented by works of painting, sculpture and stained-glass windows, is hallmarked by a profound religious feeling that had been noticed even by the ancient Romans. Art scholars evolved a notion about a distinct "German feel for form" characterized not so much by an outward beauty as by inner tension and expressiveness inherent to German art.

The gems of this section are paintings by Lucas Cranach the Elder, a great representative of the German Renaissance, who was the first to portray Venus nude and create his own type of female beauty. His painting is a combination of a classical ideal, Gothic expressiveness and an interest in minute detail inherent to the masters of Northern Europe.

Works by Ambrosius Holbein and Bartolomäus Bruyn the Elder represent the genre of portraiture that became especially widespread in Southern Germany. Their art us distinguished by a subtle skill in rendering man's inner world.

Political fragmentation, the Peasant War and a struggle of the reformation against the Church led in the middle of the sixteenth century to the disintegration of the national school. In the seventeenth century the fine arts of Germany were under a strong foreign influence. The southern areas relied mostly on Italian models, while the northern territories tended to Dutch art. Works by Christopher Paudiss and Jurgen Owens, pupils of the great Rembrandt, rank with the best paintings of this period. The second half of the eighteenth century saw the emergence of Neo-Classicism, the "spiritual father" of which is thought to have been the German art scholar Johann Joachim Winckelmann. The major artist of German Neo-Classicism was Winckelmann's friend Anton Raphael Mengs. His painting *Perseus and Andromeda* can be regarded as a pictorial implementation of Winckelmann's theory that proclaimed a return "back to antiquity".

< 170
**Unknown artist of the North German
School of the early 15th century**
*Christ at the Last Judgement with the
Interceding St Mary and St John the Baptist.*
Early 15th century. Tempera on panel.
46.5 x 70 cm. Germany

171
Stained-glass window: *St George.* **1400–10**
Coloured and transparent glass, silver etching,
overglaze colours and lead. Germany

172
**Bartolommäus Bruyn the Elder (1493–1555)
Stained-glass window:** *The Lamentation.*
Ca **1535.** Coloured and transparent glass, silver
etching, overglaze colours and lead.
174 x 87 cm. Germany

The same time also saw in Germany the flowering of portraiture that became the pride of national art. On receiving their training in Italy and France, German artists worked successfully at many European courts. This tradition was continued in the nineteenth century. Franz von Krüger became the favourite portrait painter of Nicholas I.

The mood of "elevated sorrow, a sense of "eternity and space" permeate the landscape canvases by the great nineteenth-century Romanticist Caspar David Friedrich. He never painted from life and said that the artist should pour out on to the canvas what he saw within himself. Friedrich's paintings found their way to Russia thanks to the Romantic poet Vasily Zhukovsky, who was the German artist's close acquaintance. Canvases by Hans Makart, Anselm Feuerbach, Peter von Hess and Ludwig Knauss represent German Academicism of the second half of the nineteenth century.

The pride of the collection of German art are works by the greatest artist of the twentieth century, the "father of European Abstract Art" Wassily Kandinsky, who saw the purpose of art not in imitation of nature but in the self-expression of the creative artist capable, by moving away from the shape of the object, to create "cosmic space" in colours. Kandinsky's like-minded contemporary Heinrich Campendonck worked in an outright Expressionist manner.

The German fine arts of the 1930s are represented in the Hermitage by works of Hans Grundig who sought to oppose to non-figurative painting the artistic idiom called "Expressionist Realism".

173 **Lucas Cranach the Elder (1472–1553)**
Portrait of a Woman. 1526.
Oil on panel. 88.5 x 58.6 cm. Germany

174 **Ambrosius Holbein (ca 1495 – ca 1519). *Portrait of**
a Young Man. 1518.** Oil and tempera on panel. 44 x 32.5 cm. Germany

175 > **Lucas Cranach the Elder (1472–1553)**
The Madonna and Child under the Apple-Tree. 1520s–1530s
Oil on canvas, transferred from a panel. 87 x 59 cm. Germany

176 **Jurgen Ovens (1623–1679).** *The Artist's Self-Portrait in Front of His Easel*
1670–75. Oil on canvas. 125 x 95 cm. Germany

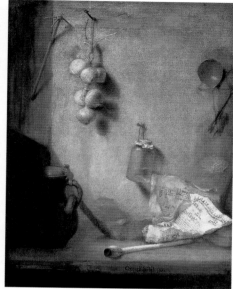

177 **Bartolommäus Bruyn the Elder (1493–1555)**
Portrait of a Man and His Three Sons.
Late 1530s – early 1540s
Oil on canvas, transferred from a panel. 75.5 x 46 cm. Germany

178 **Christopher Paudiss (*ca* 1618–1666).** *Still Life.* **1660**
Oil on canvas, transferred from a panel. 62 x 46.5 cm. Germany

179 **Bartolommäus Bruyn the Elder (1493–1555)**
Portrait of a Lady and Her Daughter.
Late 1530s – early 1540s
Oil on canvas, transferred from a panel. 75.5 x 46 cm. Germany

< 180
Anton Raphael Mengs (1728–1779)
Perseus and Andromeda. **1777**
Oil on canvas. 227 x 153.5 cm. Germany

181
Karl Friedrich Lessing (1808–1880)
The Royal Couple Mourning the Death of Their Daughter.
1830. Oil on canvas. 215 x 193 cm. Germany

< 182
Caspar David Friedrich (1774–1840).
***On a Sailing Ship. Ca* 1818–20**
Oil on canvas. 71 x 56 cm. Germany

183
Hans Makart (1840–1884). ***Female Portrait***
Third quarter of the 19th century
Oil on panel. 120 x 80 cm. Germany

184
Franz von Krüger (1797–1857)
Portrait of Prince Nikolai Saltykov
***in a Masquerade Costume.* 1850**
Oil on canvas. 98 x 79 cm. Germany

185
Anselm Feuerbach (1829–1880). ***Self-Portrait***
Oil on canvas. 92 x 73 cm. Germany

< 186
Peter von Hess (1792–1871)
Morning at Partenkirchen. **1819**
Oil on panel. 50 x 46 cm. Germany

187
Ludwig Knaus (1829–1910)
Girl in a Field. **1857**
Oil on canvas. 50 x 59 cm. Germany

188
Caspar David Friedrich (1774–1840)
The Great Mountains. Oil on canvas.
73.5 x 102.5 cm. Germany

189
Wilhelm Lachnitt (1899–1962)
Bridge. **1922.** Oil on panel.
45 x 66.5 cm. Germany

190
Hans Grundig (1901–58)
Summer Lightning over a Suburb.
1933. Oil on canvas.
76 x 93 cm. Germany

191 >
**Heinrich Kampendonk
(1889–1957)**
Man and Animals amidst Nature.
1920s. Oil on canvas.
95 x 65.5 cm. Germany

192
Wassily Kandinsky (1866–1944)
Winter. **1909.** Oil on canvas.
70 x 97 cm. Russia–Germany

193
Wassily Kandinsky (1866–1944)
View of Murnau. **1908**
Oil on canvas. 33 x 44 cm.
Russia–Germany

194
Wassily Kandinsky (1866–1944)
Landscape. **1913.** Oil on canvas.
88 x 100 cm. Russia–Germany

195
Wassily Kandinsky (1866–1944)
Composition No 6. **1913.** Oil on canvas.
194 x 294 cm. Russia–Germany

RUSSIAN CULTURE: 15TH TO EARLY 20TH CENTURY

The Hermitage collections won world-wide fame not only by exhibits from Western Europe and the East, but also by works of Russian culture that were collected and preserved in the Winter Palace literally from the first years of its existence. Some works by Russian masters decorated the state halls and living apartments of the imperial residence and some objects belonged to private collections of the Russian monarchs.

The Hermitage staff began to pay close attention to paintings by Russian artists from the early nineteenth century. In 1824 a "room of Russian painting" was opened in the building of the Hermitage; the section of Russian painting was regularly supplemented with works by academic painters. There were rooms of the Russian school in the building of the New Hermitage, too, and the central place was given to the picture *The Last Day of Pompeii* by Karl Briullov. The display also included works by Alexander Ivanov,

Fiodor Bruni and Ivan Aivazovsky. In 1898 nearly all paintings by Russian masters were transferred from the Hermitage to the Emperor Alexander III Russian Museum (now the State Russian Museum). The Hermitage, however, retained miniatures, engravings and drawings as well as superb works of Russian decorative and applied art. After 1917 works of Russian culture "migrated' from one

museum to another but eventually returned to the Hermitage – the Department of the History of Russian Culture organized in May 1941. The stocks of the young scientific department of the museum was also enriched with art objects from nationalized palaces and private collections.

Today the collection of the Department of the History of Russian Culture comprises more than 330,000 exhibits covering the period from the sixth to twentieth century and including archaeological and ethnographical materials, works of fine and decorative art and memorial objects.

A place apart is occupied by the collection of ancient Russian icons, relatively small in number, but quite significant – it includes works of major schools of icon-painting – those of Moscow, Pskov and Novgorod. The pride of the collection is the group of the so-called "northern paintings" of the thirteenth to eighteenth century, monuments of icon-painting from the Russian North. The most remarkable examples of the "northern paintings" are the early icon *The Saviour Almighty* (second half of the 13th century), the icon *The Miracle of St George and the Dragon* dating from the fifteenth or early sixteenth century, the impressive icon *The Last Judgement* painted by an anonymous artist from Kargopol in the sec-

< 196
Icon: *The Miracle of St George and the Dragon.*
Late 15th – early 16th century. Tempera on panel. 57.5 x 43 cm.
The Northern School of Icon-Painting. Russia

197
Icon: *The Last Judgement.* First half of the
16th century. Tempera on panel.
177 x 120 x 4 cm. The Novgorod school. Russia

ond half of the sixteenth century. Of great interest is the icon *St John the Theologian in Silence*, with a donative inscription on the back informing us that the image of the saint was created in 1679 by the icon-painter Grigory Kuliuksin from the Kirillo-Belozersky Monastery. One of the best icons in the Hermitage collection is the icon *St Nicholas of Zaraisk*, executed in the first half of the sixteenth century by a master of the Novgorod school – austere and restrained in style, with a characteristic inner spiritual tension of the painted image.

The Russian art school rapidly traversed in the eighteenth century a long path from a timid imitation of Western European painters to quite independent works. In the eighteenth and early nineteenth centuries the Russian art school quickly passed through all the principal phases of Western art: Baroque, Classicism and Romanticism. Ivan Vishniakov, a representative of the transitive period in Russian art of the mid-eighteenth century, combined the elements of early *parsuna* (icon-like portraits) painting with compositional devices of the French Rococo.

The bulk of the Hermitage collection consists of portraits created both by anonymous and recognized painters.

198
Icon: *St Nicholas of Zaraisk with Scenes from His Life*
First half of the 16th century. Tempera on panel.
165 x 115 x 3 cm. The Novgorod school. Russia

199
Nektary Kuliuksin. Icon:
***St John the Theologian in Silence.* 1679**
Tempera on panel. 109 x 85 x 3.5 cm. Russia

The austere and concise treatment of the sitter in combination with the exquisite colour range distinguish the portrait of Fiodor Dubiansky, the spiritual father of Empress Elizabeth painted by the well-known master of painting Alexei Antropov. Antropov's pupil Fiodor Rokotov won fame by his formal portraits.

The unique set of historical objects gives us a notion about the personality of the indefatigable Russian reformer Peter the Great and acquaints us with the age of large-scale state transformations. Beautiful memorial examples are the ship-goblet cast for Peter the Great in 1706 from the earliest silver excavated in the Transbaikal Area, in honour of Russia's victory at Gangut; his travel medicine chest executed in the seventeenth-century by German masters and the luxurious glass goblet engraved with an image of a frigate.

Rich and unusually varied is the collection of decorative and applied art, which consists of thing produced by local and foreign masters invited to Russia, where they gained a new homeland. Furniture and glass, tapestries and silver, carriages and machine-tools, bronze and porcelain, carved bone and costume – the best items from the eighteenth to early twentieth century are represented in more than 30 rooms of the Winter Palace.

200
Icon: *The Intercession*. 16th century
Tempera and gilding on panel. 74 x 51 cm. Russia

201
Icon: *Christ the Almighty*
First half of the 13th century
Tempera on panel. 64.5 x 41.5 cm.
The Northern School of Icon-Painting. Russia

202
Ivan Vishniakov (1699–1761)
Portrait of Stepanida Yakovleva. **After 1756**
Oil on canvas. 90 x 72 cm. Russia

203
Mina Kolokolnikov (*ca* 1708–1792)
Portrait of a Young Man. **1780s**
Oil on canvas. 95 x 73 cm. Russia

204
Alexei Antropov (1716–1795)
Portrait of Fiodor Dubiansky. **1761**
Oil on canvas. 99.5 x 76.5 cm. Russia

205 >
Fiodor Rokotov. *Portrait of Catherine the Great.*
1780s. Oil on canvas. 263 x 188 cm. Russia

208 >
Travel medicine set of Peter the Great.
***Ca* 1613–15.** Wood, metal, glass and
oil on copper. 39.5 x 41 x 32.5 cm. Germany

209 >
Goblet in the form of a ship. 1706
Silver-gilt. 30.5 x 12 x 37 cm. Russia

210 >
Vessel for wine. 1896–1908
Chased silver-gilt, enamel and granulation.
Height 20 cm. P. Ovchinnikov Factory, Russia

211 >
Vase. By N. S. Vereshchagin. *Ca* 1798
Walrus tusk. Height 85 cm. Russia

206
Decorative vase. 2nd quarter of the 19th century
Colourless and ruby crystal and bronze. Height 56 cm. Russia

207
Goblet. 1709–14
Glass. Yamburg Glass Works, Russia

212
**Detail of the display
"Russian Culture of the
First Half of the 18th Century"**

213
**Detail of the display
"Russian Culture of the
First Half of the 18th Century"**

214
**Detail of the display
"Russian
19th-Century Interiors".
The main drawing room
in the Empire style**

215
**Detail of the display
"Russian
19th-Century Interiors".
Drawing room
in the Art Nouveau style**

THE EASTERN COLLECTIONS

Geographically the notion of the "East" encompasses an immense area stretching from the Mediterranean coast of Africa to the Pacific Ocean. It is inhabited by numerous peoples speaking different languages and having different cultures and traditions. The collection of art of the countries of the Near and Far East number about 200,000 exhibits that entered the Hermitage in various ways: from the private collection on the royal family, as diplomatic gifts, military trophies, archaeological finds and gifts of art collectors. Many objects came to the museum after the revolution from nationalized collections and through the Purchasing Commission of the Hermitage.

The Department of the East was founded in the Hermitage in 1920. Despite its fairly brief existence, many outstanding scholars grew up here and two of them, Academicians Iosif Orbeli and Boris Piotrovsky, later became the Directors of the Hermitage.

The age of the most ancient civilizations is most fully represented in the Hermitage by Ancient Egyptian artifacts, which reflect the history of the pharaohs' country in the course of three millennia. Most of the exhibits were discovered in the tombs of pious Egyptians who believed in the miraculous force of the preserved image helping to win victory over death. It was not a mere coincidence that they called their statues the "memory of ancestors".

A notable place in the Hermitage section devoted to the cultures of Asia Minor and the Caucasus belongs to the art of Urartu, a state that had been situated on the territory of present-day Armenia and Turkey in the ninth to sixth century B.C. A pioneer in the exploration of Urartian culture is justly regarded Academician Boris Piotrovsky.

The gem of Eastern art of the Early Middle Ages is the world's best collection of silver of the Sassanian dynasty that ruled Persia from the third to seventh century. Monumental painting of this period is represented by wall paintings from the Sogdian towns of Pyanjikent and Varakhsh destroyed by the Arabs in the eighth century, and discovered by Hermitage archaeologists in the middle of the twentieth century.

The East is the area where all world religions emerged. The most ancient of them, Buddhism, is represented by fragments of wall paintings and sculpture of the fifth to tenth century from the monastery of the cave of a Thousand Buddhas discovered in the north-west of China by Academician Sergei Oldenburg in the early twentieth century. In the same period Piotr Kozlov uncovered in the deserted regions of Central Mongolia the remains of the Tangut town of Khara-Khoto destroyed by Genghis Khan in 1227. The opened burial of a noble lady yielded Buddhist icons of the eleventh to thirteenth century painted on fabric.

The superb collection of Byzantine art reflects the long history of the establishment of the Christian art canon and allows one to form an idea of the immense riches that were accumulated by the

< 216
Stele of the king's scribe Ipi.
Early 14th century B.C.
Limestone. 95 x 71 cm. Ancient Egypt

217
Statuettes of gods;
Thoth, the god of wisdom;
Anubis, the god of the dead;
Bastet, the goddess of love.
1st millennium B.C.
Bronze. Height 15.2 cm; 14 cm; 11.6 cm.
Ancient Egypt

218
Hall of Culture and Art of Ancient
Egypt: 5th millennium
B.C.– late 1st century B.C.

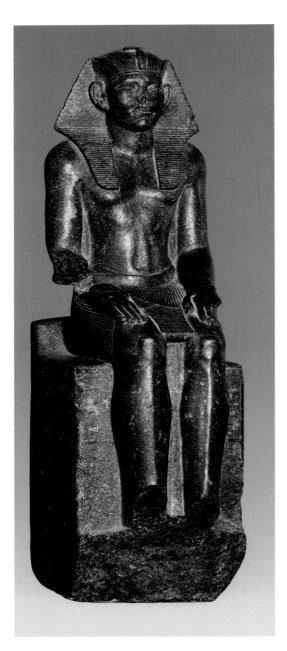

rulers of Byzantium and caused the fall of the empire. The pride of the collection are silver articles of the fifth to twelfth century discovered in burials of ancient nomads, with whom Byzantium maintained trade and diplomatic relations. Ivory objects are represented by brilliant examples of Byzantine icons, including veritable masterpieces of world significance, which are striking by their spiritual power.

The rich and varied collection of Moslem art incorporates cultural elements of the peoples subjugated by the Arabs – the Persians, Syrians and Greeks. A prohibition to depict living beings by the Koran led to an unusual flowering of ornamental art. The Hermitage's fine objects produced by Indian jewellers of the seventeenth and eighteenth centuries are decorated with colourful designs of precious stones. The Shiite movement that emerged in Islam in the seventh century recognized figurative art. The Shiite craftsmen, who lived mainly in the territory of Iran, developed the traditions of Sassanian art. The emergence of oil painting at the court of Fath Ali Shah in the nineteenth century betrays the influence of European art.

The traditional art of China and Japan is pervaded with a special contemplative world perception based on the religious notion about the necessity of man's complete union with nature. Another aspect of Oriental life is a merry and noisy character of festivities. Calm happiness and harmony characterizes landscapes, reminiscent of a beautiful dream and juxtaposing the eternal immobility of mountains with ever-changing waters. The amusing figurines of monkeys playing draughts and the lion charming for its threateningly seriousness evoke a joyful mood.

219
Statue of the Pharaoh Amenemhet III
Ca 1850–1800 B.C.
Granite. Height 86.5 cm. Ancient Egypt

220 **The outward sarcophagus of the priest Petese.
10th century B.C.** Painted wood. Height 240 cm Ancient Egypt

221 **Statuette of a priest. 15th century B.C.**
Wood. Height 34.5 cm. Ancient Egypt

222 **Figure of the cat, the sacred animal of Bastet,
the goddess of love. 1st millennium B.C.**
Bronze. Height 14 cm. Ancient Egypt

226 **Master craftsman: Ali ibn Abu-l-Kasim. Cow-shaped aquamanile. 1206** Bronze (or brass). Silver. Height 35 cm. Iran

227 **Dish with Shapur II hunting lions. 4th century.** Silver. Diameter 22.9 cm. Iran

228 **Vase with a depiction of polo playing (the *Polo Players* vase). 13th century.** Earthenware painted in lustre. Height 80 cm. Iran

< 223 *Snow Leopard Hunting.* **Wall painting of the Red Hall from the palace in the town of Varakhsh. 7th–8th century** Loess plaster, mineral paints. Height 150–200 cm. Sogdiana (Central Asia)

< 224 *Gift-Bearers.* **Wall painting. Second half of the 7th century** Loess plaster, mineral paints. 95 x 62 cm. Ajina-Tepe (Central Asia)

< 225 **Winged deity. 7th century B.C.** Bronze. Gold, ivory, stone. Height 16 cm. Urartu

229 Triptych depicting the forty martyrs of Lake Sebaste. Late 10th – early 11th century
Ivory, silver pigment. 18.5 x 24.2 cm. Byzantium

230 Casket with depictions of Hercules, centaurs and musicians
Ivory and wood. 19.5 x 28.5 x 19 cm. Byzantium

231 > **Icon:** *Christ Pantocrator. Ca* 1363
Mixed technique on panel. 106 x 79 cm. Byzantium

232 > **Icon:** *St George the Miracle-Worker.* **12th century**
Mixed technique on panel. 81 x 53 cm. Byzantium

233 > **Paten of Bishop Paternus. 491–518.** Silver-gilt with gemstones and paste. Diameter 61 cm. Byzantium

234 > **Icon:** *St John the Baptist.* **Early 14th century**
Mixed technique on panel. 66 x 39 cm. Byzantium

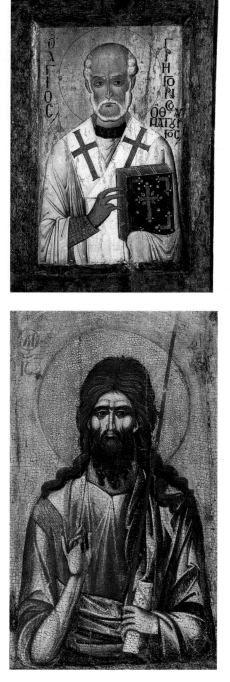

235 Unknown artist. *Dancer with Castanets.* **First quarter of the 19th century.** Oil on canvas. 158 x 90 cm. Iran

236 Lamp in a mount. Body. Egypt. Second half of the 10th century. Rock crystal. **Mount. Italy. Late 16th century** Gold and enamel. Height 26.5 cm. Length 22 cm

237 Mikhr-Ali. *Portrait of Fath Ali Shah.* **1809–10** Oil on canvas. 253 x 124 cm. Iran

238
Head of the Boddhisattva. 8th century
Earthenware, mineral colours.
Height 37 cm. Tunhuang, China

239
**The Soul of the Righteous Man Met on the Way
to the Pure Land of the Amitabkha Buddha.
Late 12th – early 13th century**
Natural colours on canvas. Khara-Khoto, Central Asia

240
**Bhaishadjaguru, the Buddha of Healing.
Late 12th – early 13th century**
Natural colours on canvas. Khara-Khoto, Central Asia

241 Tray with a depiction of a landscape. Mid-18th century
Copper painted over enamel. 18 x 18 cm. China

242 **Utagawa Hiroshige (1797–58).**
A Hundred Famous Views of Edo: Minowa and Kanasugi, Mikawashima Quarter. **1857**
Woodblock print. Japan

243 **Utagawa Hiroshige (1797–58).**
A Hundred Famous Views of Edo: Meguro. The Taiko-bashi Bridge. **1857**
Woodblock print. Japan

244 **Sinkeisai Masatoshi. Netsuke:** *Three Monkeys Playing Go*
Mid-first half of the 19th century. Ivory. 4.1 x 3.1 cm. Japan

245 **Figurine of a Lion of Fo with a pearl in its paws.**
Late 17th – early 18th century. Biscuit, enamel colours. China

246 **Screen:** *Flowers, Birds and Scenes from the Life of the*
Imperial Palace. **17th century** Detail. Mineral colours and
Coromandel lacquer on panel. 280 x 720 cm. China

< 247 **Plate. 17th century**
Gold, diamonds, rubies, emeralds and enamel.
Diameter 19.7 cm. India

< 248 **Table. 17th century**
Craftsman: Situram. Gold, diamonds, rubies,
emeralds, pearls and enamel. 27.3 x 27.3 cm. India

< 249 **Jug. 17th century**
Gold, silver, diamonds, rubies, emeralds, pearls.
Height 28.8 cm. India

250 **Jug. Body. 12th–11th century**
Rock crystal. Egypt.
Décor. 17th century
Gold and gemstones. Height 16.8 cm. Turkey

251 *Shousin, the Daos Deity of Longevity*
17th century. Gold. Height 15.5 cm. China

252 **Little bell in the shape of an eagle-warrior.**
Late 15th – early 16th century
Gold. 9 x 7.5 cm. Mexico

THE ARCHAEOLOGICAL COLLECTION

The archeological collection of the Hermitage numbers more than 500,000 exhibits representing an immense layer of human culture, from stone implements created by man 300,000 years ago to articles produced in the tenth and eleventh centuries A.D. The rich archaeological material consisting of the artifacts found during excavations, casually discovered ancient hoards and individual finds was collected on the vast expanses of the imperial, Soviet and contemporary Russia.

Russian archaeology was started by a decree of Peter the Great that ordered to send all unusual finds discovered on the territory of Russia to the Kunstkammer in St Petersburg. The issue of this decree was mainly due to the ancient golden plaques with representations of beasts discovered by Siberian treasure-seekers and presented to the Tsar by the Urals industrialist Alexei Demidov in 1715. Later these plaques had entered the famous Siberian collection of Peter the Great that was transferred from the Kunstkammer to the Imperial Hermitage in the middle of the nineteenth century.

The earliest archaeological monuments found on the territory of Russia, found their way to the Hermitage in 1812. Later the Imperial Archaeological Commission, established in 1859, sent all the best artifacts from excavations to the Imperial Museum. In 1931 the Department of Primitive Culture (now the Department of Archaeology of Eastern Europe and Siberia) was established in the Hermitage that organizes annual expeditions to various regions of the country.

The pride of place in the Hermitage's archaeological collection surely goes to the golden articles found in burial mounds of the chieftains of nomadic tribes that had inhabited the vast steppe expanses from the Danube to Mongolia.

The earliest nomads were the famous Scythians who inhabited the steppes of the Northern Black Sea Coast from the seventh to third century B.C. The ancient Scythian barrows, the first excavations of which began as early the age of Catherine the Great, yielded magnificent golden articles made in the so-called "beast style" characteristic of the nomads. A memorable image of a beast of prey, a carnivorous animal or a fantastic creature was sacred for these people and presumably personified the great powers of nature for them. Gold – the metal not affected by the course of time and resembling the sun by its glitter – was also sacred.

Starting from the seventh century B.C. the ancient Greeks settled on the northern coast of the Black Sea, built towns there and engaged in contacts with local inhabitants. Greek civilization charmed the Scythian nobility as the objects created by ancient Scythian jewellers and found in the burial mounds of rich Scythians of the fifth and fourth centuries B. C. suggest. Thanks to such masterpieces of ancient Greek metalwork as the golden comb from the Solokha barrow or the electrum vessel from the Kul-Oba burial mound, we can imagine how the Scythians, whose life, customs and legends were described by Herodotus in his *History*, looked like. The Kul-Oba

< 253
Idol. Second half of the 2nd millennium B.C.
Copper. Height 14 cm. Galich District, Kostroma Region

254
**Finial in the form of a griffin with a deer's
head in its beak. 5th–4th century B.C.**
Wood and leather. Height 23 cm. 2nd Pazyryk
burial mound. The Altai Mountains, Southern Siberia

255
**Finial in the form of the head of a griffin with a
deer's head in its beak. 5th–4th century B.C.**
Wood and leather. Height 35 cm. 2nd Pazyryk burial
mound. The Altai Mountains, Southern Siberia

256 **Pile carpet. 5th–4th century B.C.** Wool. 200 x 185 cm. 5th Pazyryk burial mound. The Altai Mountains, Southern Siberia

257 **Chariot. 5th–4th century B.C.** Wood and leather. Height 300 cm. 5th Pazyryk burial mound. The Altai Mountains, Southern Siberia

258 **Carpet. 5th–4th century B.C.** Coloured felt and appliqué work. 450 x 650 cm. 5th Pazyryk burial mound. The Altai Mountains, Southern Siberia

259 > **The display of the Department of Archaeology. 5th–4th century B.C.** 5th Pazyryk burial mound. The Altai Mountains, Southern Siberia

burial mound yielded the famous female temple pendant with a relief depicting the wise warrior Athena. It is believed that a prototype for this image was the statue of Athene Parthenos created by the great sculptor Phidias in the fifth century B.C.

In the third century B.C. the Sarmatians who came from the East ousted the Scythians. Most famous among Sarmatian burial mounds became the Khokhlach barrow of the first century A.D. that was discovered at the end of the nineteenth century not far from Novocherkassk. This barrow that yielded the golden diadem adorned with garnets, figurines of deer and a female head carved in amethyst.

The burials of nomads found in the mountain valleys of the Altai Region yielded, besides articles of precious metals, objects of wood, leather and wool produced in the fifth and fourth centuries B.C. They preserved thanks to the frost reigning at the height of more than 1,500 metres above the sea level. The richest of them was the so-called Fifth Pazyryk burial mound dug out in 1949. Dis-covered under a layer of filled earth was a log frame with a mummified body of the chieftain in a wooden sarcophagus. Next to the sarcophagus was a rolled felt carpet 30 square metres in area representing a horseman and a deity, a dismantled wooden chariot and bodies of nine horses with masks in the form of reindeer heads. The woollen pile carpet found there was evidently woven in the fifth or fourth century B.C. by craftsmen of Asia Minor and thought to be the most ancient among the carpets of this kind known today.

Many fine archaeological monuments are preserved in the Department of the History of the Ancient World. Starting from the middle of the nineteenth century, archaeologists undertake excavations of ancient Greek towns on the Northern Black Sea Coast and of necropolises lying next to them. The burial of the Bosporan king Rhescuporis III, who ruled in the third century A.D., yielded a fine golden portrait mask.

260 **Comb depicting a battle. Late 5th – early 4th century B.C.**
Gold. 12.3 x 10.2 cm. Solokha burial mound, Northern Black Sea Coast

261 **Comb. Late 5th – early 4th century B.C.**
Detail with figures of fighting Scythian warriors

262 > **Plaque in the shape of a reindeer (Kostromskaya deer). Late 7th – early 6th century B.C.**
Northern Black Sea Coast. Gold. 31.7 cm. Northern Caucasus

263 > **Vessel with a depiction of Scythian warriors. 4th century B.C.** Electrum (alloy of gold and silver).
Height 13 cm. Kul-Oba burial mound, Northern Black Sea Coast

264 > **Temple pendant with a depiction of the head of Athene Parthenos. 400–350 B.C.** Gold and enamel.
Height 18 cm. Kul-Oba burial mound, Northern Black Sea Coast

265
Diadem. 1st century. Gold, precious
and semi-precious stones, pearls and glass.
Circular length 61 cm. Height 15 cm. Khokhlach
burial mound, Northern Black Sea Coast

266
Torque 3rd–2nd century B.C.
Gold, turquoise and corals. 14.8 x 5.3 cm.
The Siberian Collection of Peter the Great

267 >
Funeral mask of a king. 3rd century
Gold. 22.5 x 15 cm. Northern Black Sea Coast

THE SMALL HERMITAGE

In 1763, still staying in Moscow after the coronation festivities, Catherine the Great expressed a desire to build in St Petersburg, next to the Winter Palace her "hermitage" – a small palace intended for her parties with a selected circle of guests. The court architect Jean-Baptiste Vallin de La Mothe worked out a preliminary project and the construction was entrusted to Yury Velten. The main feature of the Hermitage was to become the Hanging Garden raised to the height of ten metres and stretching alongside the eastern front of the Winter Palace. In 1764 Velten began to realize the project with it. A year later the Southern Pavilion intended for the apartments of Count Grigory

Orlov, the Empress's lover, was attached to the side of the Hanging Garden. Its façade overlooking Palace Square is designed in the style of Early Classicism with elements of Baroque decoration.

In 1769 the Northern or Orangery Pavilion with its front facing the Neva was put up. Designed by Vallin de La Mothe in the austere classical style, this building is on a par in its majesty with the Winter Palace. Here, on the first floor, were located the Main Hall, Orangery, Studies and the "Hermitage" – a room with lifting table for several persons. In this pavilion Catherine the Great used to arrange merry parties ending with a supper in the "Hermitage". Such parties became traditional and were named "small hermitages"; soon the entire building came to be called the Small Hermitage. The parties were held according to joking regulations compiled by the Empress herself. They prescribed not to speak Russian, to leave one's ranks and titles at the entrance, etc.

In the Main Hall of the Small Hermitage hung the paintings acquired by Catherine the Great. Very soon there was no room for them and as a result the Western and Eastern Galleries were built along-

side the Hanging Garden in 1775, which linked the Northern and Southern Pavilions of the building. Later the Western Gallery would be used for arranging portraits of the members of the ruling dynasty and it would become known as the Romanov Gallery. The Eastern Gallery would be employed for keeping the personal belongings of Peter the Great, hence her new name – the Peter Gallery.

In 1840–44, in connection with the construction of the New Hermitage, Vasily Stasov and Nikolai Yefimov reconstructed the Hanging Garden, the galleries and the Southern Pavilion.

< 268
The Small Hermitage. The Northern Pavilion
Architect: Jean-Baptiste Vallin de La Mothe. 1767–69

269
Nikolai Sablin (1736–1808).
The Hanging Garden: A Perspective View Towards the Northern Pavilion. **1773**
Engraving. Russia

270
Carl Ludwig Christineck (ca 1730 – ca 1793)
Portrait of the Architect Yury Velten.
1770s. Oil on canvas. Russia

In the 1850s Andrei Stackenschneider radically changed the layout of the Northern Pavilion. Instead of numerous rooms of the first floor he created the majestic Pavilion Hall intended for small receptions and rest. The slender marble columns, light arches, gilded moulding and iridescent crystal pendants of the chandelier turn it into one of the most magnificent interiors in the Hermitage. The decoration of the hall is greatly enhanced by its mosaic floor with representations of images of ancient Greek mythology as well as by the four marble fountains created in imitation of the Fountain of Tears in Bakhchisarai. In the Soviet period the interior was used for demonstrating the famous *Peacock* Clock made by the eighteenth-century English clock-maker James Cox and purchased by Prince Grigory Potemkin. After the death of her favourite Catherine the Great ordered to bring the clock to the Hermitage. The *Peacock* Clock became especially popular thanks to its mechanism that sometimes is put into action invariably arousing a great admiration of viewers and especially of children.

< 271
The Pavilion Hall. 1850–58.
The central section. View of the *Peacock* Clock
Architect: Andrei Stackenschneider

272
The Pavilion Hall. 1850–58.
Southern section. Mosaic inset in the floor
at the entrance to the Hanging Garden.
Decorative niche, the "Tear Fountain"

273
The *Peacock* Clock. Detail

274
**The *Peacock* Clock Mushroom
with the dial under its cap.** Detail

275 >
**The *Peacock* Clock. Made by James Cox.
Second half of the 18th century.**
Gilded bronze, silver and glass.
Height 300 cm. England

The Collection of Medieval Art

Medieval West European art of the ninth to fifteenth century, represented mainly by works of decorative and applied art, is displayed in the Western (Romanov) Gallery of the Small Hermitage. The majority of the exhibits come from the wonderful collection of Alexander Bazilewsky accumulated by him in Paris. The collection was purchased from the Russian diplomat in 1885 for 5,000,000 francs provided by Emperor Alexander III from his personal means. For a long time educated Europeans had a slighting attitude to the culture and art of the Middle Ages that had been formed as early as the Renaissance.

Medieval images, devoid of ideal beauty and full of unusual expression, seemed barbarous to the Humanists who loved Classical Antiquity. An interest in the Middle Ages emerged only in the nineteenth century when it became clear that this culture lived according to the specific laws of its own and saw a sense of earthly life in the celebration of God. This mood is reflected in art pervaded with religious symbolism.

The Middle Ages were a period when the tormenting formation of the foundations of European culture took place in the course of a thousand years. Ceaseless wars, famines and epidemics at once attacked man who saw his salvation only in God's mercy and protection. The church that took the role of both religious and political leader began to play the main role in life. All over Europe monasteries were built, which were the centres of culture for some time. A considerable role in growing towns was devoted to churches. Monastery and church treasuries preserved a great number of works of art, most of which unfortunately have not reached us. At first craftsmen active at monasteries created art objects and later urban craftsmen united into professional shops manufactured them.

The twelfth century saw an intense growth of cities and towns in France, the homeland of expressive and elegant art called "Gothic" in the nineteenth century, and a country that took a leading position in European culture. At that time the French town of Limoges became famous for its production of enamels made of variously coloured glass-like mass applied on to the surface of a metal plaque with its subsequent firing. A masterpiece in the Hermitage collection is a reliquary (a casket for keeping sacred objects and relics) with scenes from the life of the saint martyr Valeria, created in Limoges in the 1170s–1180s for King Richard the Lion-Heart. Towards the end of the twelfth century the centre of European art shifted to Paris. It was there, at the court of the King of France, who united the country, that the best architects, sculptors and craftsmen were active.

The thirteenth-century saw the flowering of the art of carving in Paris, which was due to the opening of the new trade route to western Africa that considerably increased the influx of ivory to Europe. The figurines carved of tusks were tinted with colours, gilded and were embellished with gems. Especially popular with the craftsmen was

< 276 Tapestry: *Deer Hunting*
15th – early 16th century
Wool, golden thread. 77 x 87 cm. Germany

277 Unknown craftsman. St Michael.
15th century. Wood. Height 128 cm. Netherlands

278 Aquamanile in the form of a hunting
knight. 12th or 13th century
Bronze. Height 27 cm. Hungary or Scandinavia

279 Reliquary with scenes from the life
of St Valeria. 1175. Gilded copper and enamel.
23 x 27.7 x 11.7 cm. France

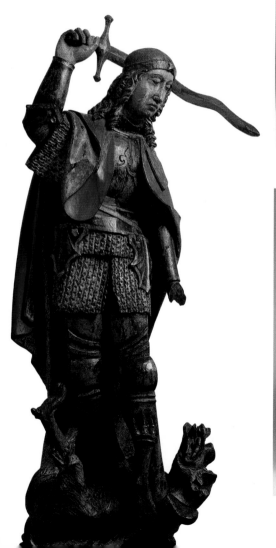

the image of the Virgin that took the features of the Fair Lady from courtoise novels and served as an object of adoration for the noble knightly estate.

Knights regarded the Archangel Michael, head of the heavenly host, traditionally depicted with arms striking the Satan, as their patron.

A special place in the Hermitage collection belongs to aquamaniles – figure-shaped metal vessels for washing hands. One of the aquamaniles is shaped like a horseman trumpeting a hunting horn, with a cheetah on horseback. This work by an anonymous craftsman was probably made in memory of the amazing beast brought from Africa.

The best ceramic ware in medieval Europe was produced in Spain, the country that had been occupied by the Moslem Arabs from the eighth to fifteenth century. Arab craftsmen decorated their faience vessels covered with white slip by lustre painting – an iridescent glaze with a gold metallic gloss. A masterpiece of Spanish-Moorish ceramics in the Hermitage is the "Fortuny Vase", produced in Malaga in the fourteenth century. The vase owes its name to the Spanish artist who found it in the nineteenth century not far from Granada. This vase for water is decorated with an Eastern pattern combined with Arabic letters. The bronze stand was made to a drawing by Fortuny himself.

Magnificent examples of medieval art are tapestries, which served both for warming and decorating, as well as various items of furniture.

280 **The Fortuny Vase. Mid-14th century** Faience, painted in lustre. Height 117 cm. **Stand. 19th century** Bronze. Spain

281 > **Processional cross with a depiction of the Last Judgement. 14th century.** Copper, silver, wood and enamel. Height 65 cm. France

282 > **The Madonna and Child. First half of the 14th century** Ebony, gilded bronze. glass and pearls. Height 22.5 cm. France

283 > **Dresser. Second half of the 15th century** Wood. 266 x 137 x 53.5 cm. France

THE NETHERLANDS: 15TH AND 16TH CENTURIES

The display of Netherlandish painting of the fifteenth and sixteenth centuries arranged in the Romanov Gallery of the Small Hermitage is not great and not of equal value. Possessing several masterpieces of a world level, the Hermitage collection does not have an opportunity to reflect Netherlandish art in all its completeness. The first large group of Netherlandish painting came to the Hermitage in 1845 with the collection of the diplomat Dmitry Tatishchev. A number of sixteenth-century Netherlandish paintings entered the Hermitage in 1915 with the collection of the geographer Piotr Semionov-Tien-Shansky sold to the museum. The Netherlandish national school of painting was born and developed in the fifteenth century, when the Dukes of Burgundy ruled the country. A remoteness from the legacy of Classical Antiquity and a religious mood made their imprint upon Netherlandish painting that retained an influence of Gothic art for a long time. The Hermitage owns five paintings by Netherlandish artists of the fifteenth century.

Robert Campin, one of the earliest Netherlandish painters, is represented by the miniature diptych *The Virgin and Child* and *The Trinity*. The work is permeated with a special pantheistic attitude to the world characteristic of northern painting, which made the artist perceive with love everything he depicted.

The picture *St Luke Painting the Virgin* by the great Rogier van der Weyden exudes lofty religious reverence. This painting was once divided into two equal parts. The right-hand part came to the Hermitage in 1850 from collection of Antoine Baer and the left-hand part in 1884 from the collection of William II of the Netherlands.

A mood of trouble and intense drama pervades the colourful altarpieces of Hugo van der Goes. Being an artist of the next generation, Goes skillfully and precisely conveys the feelings of people and demonstrates a subtle understanding of nature. The work of Gerard David completes the development of Netherlandish painting.

In the sixteenth century the Netherlands became a part of the Hapsburg world empire. Antwerp advanced to a dominant position among the cities. Cultural ties with Italy strengthened, which promoted the development of humanistic ideas and the birth of so-called "Romanism" in painting imitating Italian examples. The major representative of Italianizing painting was Marten van Heemskerk, the creator of the Hermitage triptych *The Calvary*. In his striving for intense expressiveness of sinewy naked male figures this artist vainly tried to imitate Michelangelo whom he deified.

One of the most prominent artists of the Northern Netherlands in the sixteenth century was Lucas van Leyden. Portraying people simply, without prettifying and sometimes sharply and merrily, this painter became one of the precursors of Dutch painting. His triptych *The Healing of the Blind Man of Jericho*, as experts presume, was painted for the

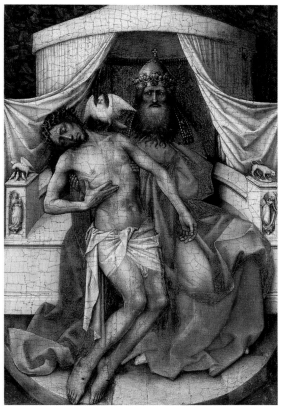

< 284 **Rogier van der Weyden (*ca* 1400–1464)** *St Luke Painting the Virgin.* **1430s.** Oil on canvas, transferred from a panel. 102.5 x 108.5 cm. Netherlands

285 **Robert Campin (*ca* 1380–1444)** *The Holy Trinity.* **1430s** Left-hand wing of a diptych. Oil on panel. 34 x 24.5 cm. Netherlands

286 **Robert Campin (*ca* 1380–1444)** *The Virgin and Child at the Fireplace* **1430s.** Right-hand wing of a diptych. Oil on panel. 34 x 24.5 cm. Netherlands

287 **Jan Mandyn. Active at Antwerp in the early 16th century.** *Landscape with the Legend of St Christopher* Oil on panel. 71 x 98.5 cm. Netherlands

288
Master of the Female Half-Lengths (Unknown Netherlandish Artist Active in the 1530s–1540s)
Female Musicians. Oil on panel. 53 x 37.5 cm. Netherlands

Leyden Hospital. Devoid of a prayerful mood, it is rather a story about a miracle performed by Jesus Christ and regarded by witnesses in a different way. The sixteenth century saw a gradual division of Netherlandish painting into different genres. There appeared artists specializing in portraiture, such as Frans Pourbus the Elder and Dirk Jacobsz, who painted group portraits popular in the middle of the sixteenth century. Landscape painting also began to develop. Artists created special "cosmic" landscapes reflecting an idea of the limitless space of the Universe. To this kind of painting may be attributed *Landscape with a Scene of the Legend about St Christopher* by Jan Mandyn. The picture featuring a powerful man named Christopher, who took death for Christ, is filled with fantastical evil creatures symbolizing human sins. The artist's style suggests the influence of the great Hieronymus Bosch.

The Hermitage does not possess works by Pieter Brueghel the Elder. Visitors can form an idea of the light and joyful art of this outstanding master from copies executed by his son and pupil, Pieter Brueghel the Younger. Human figurines in Brueghel's paintings are reminiscent of a multicoloured mosaics with the perfectly painted landscape serving as its background.

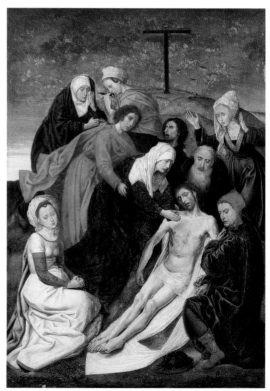

291 **Frans Pourbus the Elder (1545–1581)**
***Portrait of a Man*. 1570s.** Oil on panel. 87 x 78 cm

292 **Hugo van der Goes (*ca* 1440–1482).**
***The Lamentation*. 1470s**
Oil on panel. 36.2 x 30.2 cm. Netherlands

< 291 **Master of the Female Half-Lengths (Unknown Netherlandish Artist Active in the 1530s–1540s)** *The Madonna and Child* Oil on panel. 53.2 x 42.4 cm. Netherlands

292 **Hugo van der Goes (ca 1440–1482)** *The Adoration of the Magi* **1470s.** Triptych. Oil on canvas, transferred from a panel. Central part. 96.3 x 77 cm. Side wings: 96.2 x 31.7 cm. Netherlands

293 **Gerard David (ca 1460–1523)** *St Mary Embracing the Dead Christ* **Late 15th century** Oil on panel. 36 x 44.5 cm. Netherlands

Lucas van Leyden (1489/94–1533). *The Healing of the Blind Man of Jericho.* **1531**
Triptych. Oil on canvas; transferred from a panel. Central part: 115.5 x 150.5 cm. Side wings: 89 x 33.5 cm. Netherlands

295 **Marten van Heemskerk (1498–1574)**
The Calvary. **1543 (?).** Triptych. Oil on canvas; transferred from a panel. Central part: 100.7 x 58.3 cm. Side wings: 100 x 28 cm. Netherlands

296 **Kerstiaen de Keunick (*ca 1560–ca 1635*)**
Landscape with Tobias and the Angel
Oil on panel. 40 x 63 cm. Netherlands

297 > **Pieter Brueghel the Younger (*ca 1564–1638*)** *The Adoration of the Magi*
Oil on canvas, transferred from a panel.
36 x 56 cm. Netherlands

298 > **Pieter Brueghel the Younger (*ca 1564–1638*)**
Fair with a Theatrical Performance
Oil on panel. 110 x 164.5 cm. Netherlands

The Large (Old) Hermitage. The Hermitage Theatre

In 1771, simultaneously with the construction of the two galleries of the Small Hermitage, Yury Velten began to put up on the Palace Embankment a new building for housing art collections and libraries. Called later the Large (or Old) Hermitage, this block was created in several phases. In 1775 its western half, connected by an arched passage with the Northern (La Motte's) Pavilion of the Small Hermitage was completed. The principal interior of the new building was the Oval Hall richly adorned with columns, moulding and the ceiling painting *The Virtues Presenting Russian Youth to Minerva* by the French painter Gabriel François Doyen. Under the Oval Hall was located a small theatre for performances held during Catherine's "small hermitages".

In 1777 the construction of the eastern section of the Large Hermitage began and as a result the building stretched alongside the Neva embankment up to the Winter Canal. The construction of the Large Hermitage was entirely completed in 1787. The décor of its austere, concise front was to emphasize the pow-

erful beauty of the Northern Pavilion and the plastic expressiveness of the Winter Palace. The inner decoration, in contrast, was distinguished by luxury and elegance befitting as a background for the collections of the Empress. Catherine the Great held "large hermitages" several times a year in this building inviting up to 200 guests.

Emperor Nicholas I ordered to bring all the art collections to the New Hermitage, and in 1851 his favourite architect Andrei Stackenschneider began to work on the reconstruction of the Large (Old) Hermitage and the work lasted for nearly ten years. The ground floor was allotted to the State Council and the Council of Ministers. On the first floor a suite of state rooms for the heir to the throne Nikolai Alexandrovich, the elder son of Emperor Alexander II was created. In the decoration of the halls the designer amply used gilding, coloured stones, precious kinds of wood, moulding and painting. The Main Staircase should be recognized as Stackenschneider's best creation in the Large Hermitage. Called the Council

Staircase as it was located near the vestibule of the hall where sessions of the State Council were held, the staircase was richly embellished with natural and artificial marble. Its ceiling is adorned with the painting by Gabriel François Doyen that had decorated the Oval Hall.

In 1775 Catherine the Great received as a gift tinted engravings reproducing frescos of the famous Vatican Loggias created by Raphael with his pupils in the early sixteenth century.

< 299 **Karl Beggrow**
(from the original by Sabbath and Chifflard).
Watercolour with a view of the Old Hermitage. 1826. Russia

300 **D. Polly.** ***Portrait of Architect Giacomo Quarenghi***
1810s. Oil on canvas

301 **Carl Collmann.** ***View of the Hermitage Theatre***
and the Arch Across the Winter Canal. **1820s**
Lithograph from a watercolour

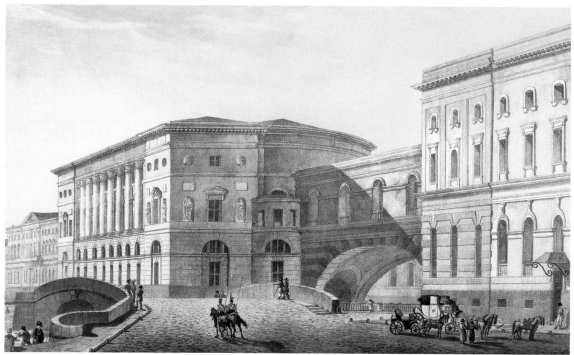

The Empress expressed a desire to have their life-size copies. The copying in tempera on canvas was entrusted to the Rome-based artist Christoph Unterberger who carried out this work together with V. Peter in Rome in 1778–85. Originally it was planned to arrange the paintings in the halls of the Winter Palace. In 1779, however, the Italian architect Giacomo Quarenghi suggested an idea to build a special block next to the Large Hermitage. The construction of the Loggias Block, started in 1783, was completed only nine years later. The Raphael Loggias themselves form a gallery ninety metres long divided by pillars into thirteen equal sections each of which is covered by a square vault and separated from the others by a semicircular arch. Represented on the vaults are biblical scenes, while the walls and pillars are decorated with whimsical grotesques.

In the 1840s, in connection with a start of the construction of the New Hermitage, the Raphael Loggias Block was dismantled and the canvases bearing the paintings, as well as the mirrors, doors and parquet floors were removed, preserved and used again in the complex of the halls of the new museum.

In November 1783 Quarenghi received a commission for the construction of a new theatre in the former Winter Palace of Peter the Great behind the Winter Canal. Yury Velten was entrusted to create a structure "for a passage to the theatre across the canal through a gallery". Taking into consideration a short time and a shortage of funds given for the construction, Quarenghi retained the basement and walls of Peter's palace building the stage and auditorium inside. The first performance was held there on 16 November 1785. Although decoration work was still under way, performances in the new theatre were held one or two times a week. The building of the theatre took its final shape in 1789, when on the Neva embankment there appeared a simple and harmonious façade decorated with columns and statues of ancient Greek poets and playwrights. The decoration of the auditorium built as an amphitheatre adorned with columns, statues of Apollo and the Muses and medallions with profile portraits of famous dramatists is also sustained in the classical traditions.

302
The Hall of Italian Primitives. 1851–58.
Architect: Andrei Stackenschneider

303 >
The Leonardo da Vinci Room. 1858–60.
Architect: Andrei Stackenschneider

< 304 **The Hermitage Theatre. The auditorium. 1783–85**

305 **Concesio Albani (?–1818)**
Statue of a Muse. **1784–85.** Marble. Italy

**306 The Raphael Loggias.
Biblical scenes and ornamental
compositions. 1778–85**
Painting of the vault. Christoph
Unterberger, B. Peter. Tempera on canvas

307 The Raphael Loggias. 1778–85
The Last Supper
Painting of the vaulted bay.
Artists: Christopher Unterberger,
B. Peter. Tempera on canvas

308 > The Raphael Loggias
Architect: Giacomo Quarenghi.
1783–92. Copy of the Loggias from
the Papal Palace in the Vatican.
Incorporated into the building
of the New Hermitage in 1841–51

ITALY: 13TH TO 16TH CENTURY

The halls of the Large (Old) Hermitage are devoted to the display of Italian art of the thirteenth to sixteenth century, the time of the burgeoning and flowering of the Renaissance, a great period in the history of Western Europe.

The formation of this collection began in the last quarter of the eighteenth century by Catherine the Great. One of the most important acquisitions was the Paris collection of Baron Pierre Crozat (1772). In 1850 the Italian collection of the Hermitage was enriched with paintings from the Venetian Palace of the Barbarigo family. In the second half of the nineteenth century veritable masterpieces – *The Litta Madonna* by Leonardo da Vinci and *The Conestabile Madonna* by Raphael –were bought in Italy. In the early twentieth century the Hermitage acquired *The Madonna* by Simone Martini and *The Madonna with a Flower (The Benois Madonna)* by Leonardo da Vinci. After the revolution of 1917 the Italian collection grew mainly owing to the nationalization of private collections, of which the most prominent was the assemblage of early Italian art received from the Stroganov Museum.

Art of the thirteen and fourteenth centuries, called Proto-Renaissance art, is represented by religious paintings following the medieval tradition: a conventional background, figures depicted on a different scale and anatomical distortions. A masterpiece of the Hermitage collection of this period is *The Madonna* from *The Annunciation* diptych by the eminent Sienese master Simone Martini. This is the right-hand wing of a folding altarpiece divided at some later date. The left-hand wing depicting the Archangel Gabriel can be found in the National Gallery of Art in Washington.

The cradle of the Italian Renaissance was proud, independent Florence. It was there that man, who started thinking of himself as a great creator and the centre of the Universe, became the main theme in art for the first time in new history. A new notion found a corresponding implementation in man's ideal image that had been created earlier by Classical Antiquity and now became the basic school for Italian artists.

In the fifteenth century, the period of the Early Renaissance, Florentine artists were the first artists in Italy to solve the task of a faithful depiction of the real world using the laws of linear and aerial perspective. They studied anatomy to correctly paint the human body – the most beautiful natural form. In the Hermitage this period is represented by works of the sublime Fra Beato Angelico, the subtle lyrical painter Filippino Lippi, the contemplative Perugino and many other artists. The paintings by Sandro Boticelli, the most prominent artist of the Quattrocento, reflect the period when he was under the influence of the religious preacher Girolamo Savonarola who called to deny earthly joys.

The period of the highest flowering of Renaissance art, the High Renaissance, covers a little more than two decades at the turn of the fifteenth and sixteenth centuries. It was in this period that Leonardo da Vinci, Michelangelo and Raphael created their best works. The works by Michelangelo and

< 309 **Fra Beato Angelico da Fiesole (*ca* 1400–1455)**
The Madonna and Child with Angels. Ca 1425
Tempera on panel. 81 x 51 cm. Italy

310 **Niccolo di Pietro Gerini (mentioned from 1368 to 1415)**
The Crucifixion with St Mary and St John. 1390–95
Tempera on panel. 85.5 x 52.7 cm. Italy

311 **Simone Martini (*ca* 1284–1344).** *The Madonna from
The Annunciation scene. Ca* 1340–1344. Right-hand wing
of a folding icon. Tempera on panel. 30.5 x 21.5 cm. Italy

312 **Antonio da Firenze (active in the first half of the
15th century).** *The Madonna and Child with Saints
On the reverse:* *The Crucifixion with St Mary and St John*
Tempera on panel. 151.5 x 84.5 cm. Italy

< 313
Leonardo da Vinci (1452–1519)
The Madonna with a Flower
(The Benois Madonna). **1478**
Oil on canvas, transferred from a panel.
49.5 x 33 cm. Italy

314
Filippino Lippi (1457–1504)
The Adoration of the Infant Christ. **Mid-1480s**
Oil on copper plate, transferred from a panel.
Diameter 53 cm. Italy

Raphael are exhibited in the New Hermitage. Leonardo's paintings can be seen in the vastest interior of the Large Hermitage, now known as the Leonardo da Vinci Room. Each Leonardo work, and just about a dozen of them have survived to this day, is a great marvel. The man of universal genius, who left a trace in all spheres of human culture, Leonardo da Vinci was not excelled in painting. Leonardo's contemporaries, looking at the images "getting alive" in his pictures, did not believe that a usual man could create them. The Hermitage owns two masterpieces of the great master – *The Madonna with a Flower* painted in 1478, was acquired by the museum in Florence in 1914 from the collection of the Benois family, and *The Madonna and Child*, created by the artist in the 1490s in Milan, was purchased by the Hermitage in 1865 from Count Antonio Litta.

A place apart in Italian art of the Renaissance Age belongs to Venice. Until the tenth century this city was controlled by the Byzantine Empire. On becoming free, the Venetian Republic grew into the wealthiest European state. Members of the Vene-

tian nobility were ready to do anything in order to enlarge the wealth and grandeur of their city. This striving for luxury was reflected in such vivid and colourful art as the Venetian carnival. The novel, Renaissance tendencies appeared in Venetian painting only in the second half of the fifteenth century. The Venetian artists succeeded to make up for lost time, and in the sixteenth century the Venetian school became one of the leading schools in Italy. Among its representatives were such excellent painters as Giorgione, who created the famous painting *Judith*, on the best in the collection of the museum and his great pupil Titian. The latter is represented in the Hermitage collection by eight canvases, including veritable masterpieces of world significance: *Danaë*, whose image Titian painted several times, *The Repentant Mary Magdalene* and *St Sebastian*. One of Titian's most talented pupils, Paolo Veronese, was the author of the mournful painting *The Lamentation*.

Female Portrait by Correggio, the major Parma painter, belongs to masterpieces of Italian portrait painting in the collection of the Hermitage.

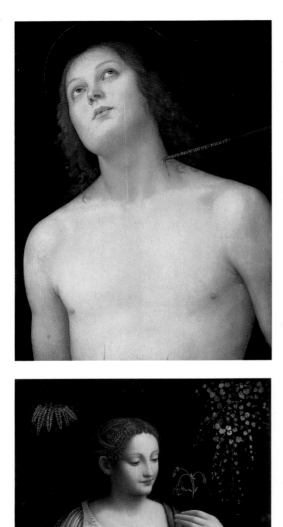

315 **Leonardo da Vinci (1452–1519).** *The Madonna and Child (The Litta Madonna). Ca* **1490–91.** Tempera on canvas, transferred from a panel. 42 x 33 cm. Italy

316 **Perugino (Pietro Vannucci) (1450–1523)** *St Sebastian. Ca* **1495.** Oil on panel. 53.5 x 39.5 cm. Italy

317 **Sandro Botticelli (1445–1510).** *St Dominic* **Early 1490s.** Oil on canvas, transferred from a panel. 44.5 x 26 cm. Italy

318 > **Francesco Melzi (1493–1570).** *Female Portrait (Flora). Ca* **1520.** Oil on canvas. 76 x 63 cm. Italy

319 **Veronese (Paolo Caliari) (1528–1588).**
The Lamentation. **Between 1576 and 1582.**
Oil on canvas. 147 x 111.5 cm. Italy

320 > **Correggio (Antonio Allegri)
(1489/1504–1534).** *Female Portrait. Ca* **1519.**
Oil on canvas. 103 x 87.5 cm. Italy

321 > **Giorgione (Giorgio da Castelfranco)
(ca 1478–1510).** *Judith.* **Early 1500s** Oil on canvas,
transferred from a panel. 144 x 68 cm. Italy

322 > **Domenico Capriola (1494–1528).**
Portrait of a Man. **1512**
Oil on canvas. 117 x 85 cm. Italy

‹ 323 **Titian (Tiziano Vecellio)**
(1485/90–1576). *Danaë.* **Between 1546 and 1553**
Oil on canvas. 120 x 187 cm. Italy

‹ 324 **Titian (Tiziano Vecellio) (1485/90–1576)**
Christ the Almighty. Ca **1570**
Oil on canvas. 96 x 80 cm. Italy

‹ 325 **Titian (Tiziano Vecellio) (1485/90–1576)**
Portrait of a Young Woman. Ca **1536**
Oil on canvas. 96 x 75 cm. Italy

326 **Titian (Tiziano Vecellio) (1485/90–1576)**
Repentant Mary Magdalene. **1560s**
Oil on canvas. 119 x 97 cm. Italy

THE WINTER PALACE OF PETER THE GREAT

The basement rooms of the Hermitage Theatre house perhaps the most unusual exhibition of the museum – the historical, architectural and memorial complex "the Winter Palace of Peter the Great". This building has disappeared from the plans of St Petersburg back in the eighteenth century, but thanks to sensational discoveries of the Hermitage scholars a visit to the palace and a tour of it rank with the most popular tourist routes in the museum. In the middle of the 1980s, during the reconstruction of the Hermitage Theatre were found sizeable architectural fragments dating from the first quarter of the eighteenth century. It turned out that the Hermitage Theatre erected by the outstanding architect Giacomo Quarenghi for Catherine the Great at the end of the eighteenth century, engulfed the walls of the structured built in the age of Peter the Great.

Peter had no permanent dwelling in St Petersburg for quite a long time. It was only in the spring of 1708 that a one-storeyed wooden house with a mezzanine, completed by a pediment and a spire, suitable for winter, was built on Admiralty Island, approximately on the site where the Winter Canal discharges its waters into the Neva. The house had merely ten small rooms, two of which were allotted for the Tsar's favourite pastimes: "for turning portraits and figures" on a lathe and for making models of ships.

As early as 1711 Alexander Menshikov received an order to dismantle the "small chambers of the Winter Palace" and to begin the construction of new chambers for the Tsar. Less than in a year Peter had a befitting winter house, one of the largest among the first stone structures in St Petersburg of the early eighteenth century. On 19 February 1712 the Tsar's new palace designed by Dominico Trezzini and later called the "Wedding Chambers" became the setting of the ceremony held on occasion of Peter's marriage to Catherine. The second Winter Palace, however, could not meet everyday and "representative" demands – there was no room for tutors of the Tsar's children and the Tsarina's numerous servants, no room for arranging assemblies and for receptions of envoys of foreign states.

A project of the third Winter House was worked out by Georg Johann Mattarnovy, who began its erection in 1716. The final phase of the construction work in 1719–24 was directed by Dominico

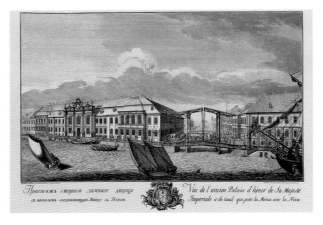

Проспектъ стараго зимняго дворца съ каналами соединяющими Мойку съ Невою

Vue de l'ancien Palais d'hiver de Sa Majesté Imperiale et du Canal qui joint la Moica avec la Neva

Trezzini. In the autumn of 1723 the building was mainly completed. In the centre of the horizontally extended façade was arranged a majestic portal resembling a triumphal arch. The luxurious attic was embellished with statues and relief allegorical compositions. The building was located closer to the Neva, so that the "Wedding Chambers" turned out to be in the depth of the Tsar's plot of land.

The block overlooking the Neva was adjoined on the side of the Winter Canal by the so-called "Small Chambers" used as the Sovereign's private apartments. They bordered with a small colourful garden

< 327 *Perspective View of the Old Winter Palace (The Winter Palace of Peter the Great).* **1753**
Engraving by Grigory Kachalov from a drawing by Mikhail Makhayev

328 **Bartolomeo Carlo Rastrelli (1645–1744).**
The posthumous figure of Peter the Great.
1725. Wax on wood. Height 204 cm. Russia

having a fountain in its centre; further on there was a harbour for small vessels and a slipway.

In the inner decoration of the dwelling apartments and state rooms of the palace were widely employed fabrics, tapestries, morocco, Dutch tiles and artificial marble. The oak doors and window surrounds were lined with canvas and cloth; the parquet floors were made of oak, walnut and maple. The building had comfortable systems of heating and sewage.

Peter lived and worked in the third Winter Palace during his later years and he died here on 28 January 1725. The imperial residence stood intact for two more years under Catherine I; after her death musicians, dancers, cobblers and merchants inhabited the building; in the reign of Elizabeth Petrovna it was used as barracks. On 6 November 1783 Catherine the Great signed a decree about the construction of a court theatre on the site of Peter's dilapidated residence. Quarenghi, however, left the former foundation and partly the old walls owing to a shortage of funds and limited time given for the construction work.

Thanks to that under the auditorium of the Hermitage Theatre there survived intact the walls of the ground floor of the "Small Chambers". This enabled to re-create several interiors of the Petrine age – the Turnery, the Study and the Dining Room – in the former apartments of the Emperor. Placed there were the lathe and tools used by Peter the Great as well as various articles he turned of wood and bone, his walking-sticks and spectacles, furniture, a superb clock with musical mechanism, the stuffed dummy of one of the Tsar's dogs and the landscapes and still lifes acquired by Peter the Great in Western Europe. Displayed in the main courtyard is the Emperor's carriage. In the former Corps de Guards Room one can see the now famous "Wax Effigy" created after the Emperor's death by the court sculptor Bartolomeo Carlo Rastrelli.

329
The roundabout gallery and the inner courtyard. The carriage of Peter the Great and a masquerade sledge

330 >
The Dining Room. Detail of the display

THE NEW HERMITAGE

The last building in the series of structures of the Imperial Hermitage was the New Hermitage, unusual for St Petersburg architecture, as it was specially intended for keeping art collections. A decision to build the "Imperial Public Museum" was taken by Nicholas I during the re-creation of the Winter Palace after the devastating fire of 1837. In May 1839, at the Emperor's invitation, a specialist in museum architecture, the famous German architect Leo von Klenze came to Russia. It took him merely two months to create a project for the new Klenze, who offered, for instance, to demolish the block of the Large (Old) Hermitage.

The construction of the New Hermitage was carried out from 1842 to 1851 under the supervision of Vasily Stasov until his very death in 1848. His main assistant Nikolai Yefimov completed the construction work. Leo von Klenze himself, staying in Munich, watched the construction by correspondence and coming to Russia from time to time. In September 1850 the building was officially named the New Hermitage and the ceremony of

building. At the same time the Special Commission for the Building of the Museum was formed. It included the foremost architects Vasily Stasov, Alexander Briullov and Nikolai Yefimov. In the process of preliminary work Stasov and Yefimov made substantial amendments to the project of Leo von

the inauguration of the museum was held on 5 February 1852.

As a representative of the age of the Historical style, Leo von Klenze succeeded in blending in his project elements of diverse styles – those of Classical Antiquity, Renaissance and Baroque. But the dominant role in the design of the building was given to Classicism. The two-storeyed building with protruding three-storeyed pavilions, reminiscent of mighty fortress bastions, instills a feeling of grandeur and calm. The smooth walls of the structure are adorned with classical ornaments and statues of outstanding art figures from different periods: Phidias, Leonardo da Vinci, Rembrandt and others. The accent of the main façade overlooking Million-naya Street is the famous portico with ten figures of granite Atlantes created by the sculptor Alexander Terebenev. The inner décor of the halls and rooms of the New Hermitage amazes us by its variety and opulence. The series of interiors opens up with a vestibule decorated by red granite columns, from which the suites of state rooms diverge to the left and right. Their vaults are covered with moulded decoration, the walls are trimmed with colourful artificial marble and marble slabs cover the floors. Formerly these interiors were employed to accommodate the collection of ancient and new sculpture and a library. Today the ground floor of the New Hermitage serves for the display of ancient art. The most famous interior is the Twenty-Column Hall or the Hall of Greek-Etruscan Vases that is reminiscent of an ancient Greek temple in its appearance. Twenty granite columns divide the hall into three sections, the floor is covered with mosaics of various kinds of marble; the walls bear panels with copies of paintings from ancient Greek vases.

In one of the halls of the ground floor, among ancient busts, stands the famous Kolyvan Vase, one of the largest stone vases in the world. Altai stonecutters in the middle of the nineteenth century carved it of Revniukha jasper.

The majestic marble Main Staircase, decorated with a monumental granite colonnade, leads from the vestibule to the first floor of the New Hermitage. The rooms of the first floor are embellished with columns, gilded moulding, wall painting, sumptu-

ous furniture and rich parquet floors. The pride of place is given in the New Hermitage to articles of coloured stone – decorative vases, standard lamps and tables produced by Russian master craftsmen in the eighteenth and nineteenth centuries at the Peterhof, Yekaterinhof and Kolyvan Lapidary Works to projects by the brilliant architects Giacomo Quarenghi, Andrei Voronikhin and others.

The landing of the first floor adjoins the Gallery of the History of Ancient Painting. Eighty pictures painted in wax colours on copper plates decorate the walls and domes of this gallery. They illustrate

< 331 **Luigi Premazzi (1814–1891).**
View of the New Hermitage from the South-East.
1861. Watercolour. 32 x 43.6 cm. Italy

332 **Portico with Atlantes (1842–51). Architect:**
Leo von Klenze. Sculptor: Alexander Terebenev
(1815–1859). 1840s. Serdobolye granite

the history of painting reflected in myths and legends of the ancient Greeks. Nowadays the Gallery us used for the display of Western European sculpture from the age of Neo-Classicism.

Several halls stand out in appearance among the similar interiors running around the perimeter of the entire building. These are the three magnificent top-lighted interiors, known as skylight halls, which were created specially for a display of large-scale paintings.

An original decorative device was used in the design of the Tent-Shaped Hall, the gabled ceiling of which reveals the system of supporting rafters covered with painting. An elaborate organization of space distinguishes the Twelve-Column Hall with its upper gallery and loggias.

The halls of the first floor, intended mainly for showing Western European art, had contained before 1898 pictures by Russian painters, too. The Twelve-Column Hall was employed for the display of numismatic collections from the Munzkabinett. Today all these interiors show the objects created in Western Europe between the fifteenth and nineteenth centuries. Particularly popular, especially with younger visitors, is the Knights' Hall where the most artistic examples of arms and armour produced by Western European masters from the fifteenth to seventeenth century are displayed.

< 333 **The Main Staircase of the New Hermitage. 1842–51.** Architect: Leo von Klenze

334 **Upper landing of the Main Staircase of the New Hermitage. 1842–51.** Architect: Leo von Klenze

339
The Small Italian Skylight Hall. 1842–51
Architect: Leo von Klenze

340 > **Eduard Hau (1816–1895). *The Hall of the Spanish School*. 1856.** Watercolour. 33.5 x 42.1 cm. Russia

341 > **Table with lapis-lazuli top. 1850s**
Badakhshan lapis lazuli and ormolu. 110 x 220 cm. Russia

342 **The Van Dyck Room. Display of Flemish art of the 17th and 18th centuries. 1842–51.** Architect: Leo von Klenze

343 > **The Snyders Room. Display of Flemish art of the 17th and 18th centuries. 1842–51.** Architect: Leo von Klenze

< 344 **The Tent-Shaped Hall. The display of Dutch 17th-century art. 1842–51** Architect: Leo von Klenze

346 **The display of Dutch 17th-century art.** Detail

345 **Luigi Premazzi (1814–1891). The Hall of the Dutch and Flemish Schools. 1858.** Watercolour. 29.2 x 41.9 cm. Italy

< 347 **The Knight's Hall. The display of Western European arms and armour of the 15th to 17th century. 1842–51.** Architect: Leo von Klenze

348 **The Knight's Hall. "The Cavalcade of Knights"**

349 **The Knight's Hall. Helmet. 1530–40**
Master craftsman: Filippo Negroli (?). Gilded steel. Italy

350
The Gallery of the History of Ancient Painting. Detail of the painted décor. Encaustics (wax colours on copper)

351
The Gallery of the History of Ancient Painting *Portrait of the Architect Leo von Klenze* Detail of the moulded decoration of the ceiling

352 >
The Gallery of the History of Ancient Painting. 1842–51. Architect: Leo von Klenze

< 353 *Flora.* **Sculptor: Pietro Tenerani.**
1840. Marble. Height 163 cm. Italy

< 354 **The Gallery of the**
History of Ancient Painting
Detail of the painted décor. Encaustics

< 355 **Antonio Canova (1757–1822)**
The Three Graces. **1813**
Marble. Height 182 cm

356 **The Gallery of the**
History of Ancient Painting
Architect: Leo von Klenze

357 *Cupid and Psyche*
Sculptor: Antonio Canova. 1796
Marble. Height 137 cm. Italy

< 358
The Twenty-Column Hall. 1842–51
Architect: Leo von Klenze

359
Konstantin Ukhtomsky (1818–1881).
The Hall of Greek-Etruscan Vases. 1853
Watercolour. 29.2 x 41.6 cm. Russia

360
The Hall of the Kolyvan Vase. 1842–51
Architect: Leo von Klenze
The Kolyvan Vase. 1829–43
To a design by Avraam Melnikov.
Revniukha jasper. Height 257 cm. Russia

361
Hall of Greek Art of the 5th Century B.C. (Hall of Athene). 1842–51. Architect: Leo von Klenze

362
Portrait of the Roman Emperor Antoninus Pius. 2nd century. Marble. Rome

363 >
A Roman courtyard. Display of Roman decorative sculpture of the 1st and 2nd centuries. 1842–51
Architect: Leo von Klenze

364
The Hall of Dionysus (Hall of Venus).
The display of Greek art: 4th to 1st century B.C. 1842–51
Detail. Architect: Leo von Klenze

< 365 **The Hall of Dionysus (Hall of Venus).**
Aphrodite (Venus of Tauris). Roman copy
from the Greek original of the 3rd century B.C.
Marble. Height 169 cm. Rome

366 **The Hall of Dionysus (Hall of Venus).**
The display of Hellenistic art:
4th to 1st century B.C. 1842–51
Detail. Architect: Leo von Klenze

367
**Hall of Greek Art
of the 14th to 5th Century B.C.
(Hall of the Archaic Period). 1842–51**
Architect: Leo von Klenze

368
**The Hall of the
Archaic Period.
Greek ceramics of the
7th and 6th B.C.**

369 >
The Hall of the Archaic Period
Detail of the display

< 370
***Jupiter.* 1st century A.D.**
Marble and tinted plaster.
Height 347 cm. Rome

371
The Hall of Jupiter. 1842–51
Architect: Leo von Klenze.

372
Luigi Premazzi (1814–1891)
The Hall of Newest Sculpture. **1856**
Watercolour. 29.8 x 42 cm. Italy

373
The Hall of Art of the Hellenistic Age
Detail of the decoration. Architect: Leo von Klenze

374
Konstantin Ukhtomsky (1818–1881).
The Hall of the Antiquities
of the Cimmerian Bosporus. **1854**
Watercolour. 37.8 x 30.6 cm. Russia

375 >
The Hall of Art of the Hellenistic Age
(the former Hall of the Antiquities
of the Cimmerian Bosporus).
3rd to 1st century B.C. 1842–51
Architect: Leo von Klenze

ART OF CLASSICAL ANTIQUITY

The Hermitage possesses a fine collection of ancient art covering the period from the eighth century B.C. to the fourth century A.D. Its best examples occupy nearly twenty rooms in the New Hermitage. The first ancient works, including the famous statue of Aphrodite (Venus of Tauride) appeared in Russia in the age of Peter the Great. They adorned the Summer Gardens, the Kunstkammer and palaces of the new Russian capital. Catherine the Great bought works by ancient artists with her characteristic sweep, although the majority of the marble statues were sent to the suburban residences – Tsarskoye Selo, Pavlovsk and Gatchina. In her "hermitage" the Empress preferred to keep her favourite ancient gems.

Worthy of special mention among the Empress's acquisitions were the collection of sculpture of the Englishman John Lyde Browne (1785). In the nineteenth century the Hermitage received large collections of classical art acquired from the Roman art collector Pizzati (1834), Comtesse de Lavalle (1851) and the proprietor of foundries Demidov (1852). In 1814 Joséphine de Beauharnais presented to Emperor Alexander I the world-famous gem dating from the third century B.C., the so-called "Gonzaga Cameo". The most considerable acquisition was made in 1861, when the best part of the huge ancient collection of Marquis Gian Pietro Campana entered the Imperial Museum.

In the first half of the nineteenth century there also appeared a new source for the enrichment of the stocks of Classical Antiquity – regular excavations of ancient Greek settlements started on the Northern Black Sea Coast. After the revolution the Hermitage assemlage was augmented due to the nationalization of private collections. At the present time objects of ancient culture enter the Hermitage basically through its purchasing commission.

Art of Ancient Greece and Rome, called "ancient art" in the age of the Renaissance, has a special significance for Europe, because Classical Antiquity is the cradle of European civilization. The ancient Greek philosopher Protagoras, who proclaimed man as the measure of all things, most exactly expressed the basis of ancient world perception. The main task of ancient art was the creation of an ideally beautiful man. Great creations of Ancient Greece and Rome have for ever become unrivalled examples for the generations to come. Therefore ancient art is recognized in Europe as classical art.

The Hermitage's ancient collection allows one to trace the path traversed by man towards the understanding of his grandeur. Greek sculpture is represented in the museum mainly by marble copies created in Ancient Rome at the turn of the old and new era. But even copies enable us to appreciate the great alterations that took place in ancient Greek art from the sixth to first century B.C., from the time of timid schooling in the archaic period to the virtuoso mastery in the age of Hellenism.

The Hermitage's collection of ancient ceramics is one of the best in the world. Encompassing a period of a thousand years, it is represented by a great variety of objects, from the most ancient vessels painted in the austere geometrical style to Corinthian vases of different shapes covered with

< 376 **Cameo:** *Ptolemy II and Arsinoë II*
(the Gonzaga Cameo) 3rd century B.C.
Sardonix. 15.7 x 11.8 cm. Alexandria

377 **Hydria with a scene of Eleusinian mysteries**
(the Queen of Vases). 4th century B.C.
Painted and gilded earthenware. Height 62.2 cm. Campana

378 **Lekythos in the shape of a sphinx.**
Late 5th century B.C.
Painted and gilded earthenware. Height 21.5 cm. Attica

379 **Funeral urn. Mid-4th century B.C.**
Bronze. Height 42 cm.
Length of the platform 69 cm. Etruria

luxurious "carpet-like" patterns. Among a great number of black- and red-figure Attic vases of the sixth and fifth centuries B.C. there are superb examples created by the foremost masters from Athens. They were found in all the places where the Hellenes then settled establishing their towns-colonies. A veritable masterpiece of the Hermitage's collection of ancient ceramics is justly regarded the hydria known as the "Queen of Vases" and executed in the fourth century B.C. by an unknown Greek master living in the area of Campania in Ancient Italy. No less famous is the sphinx-shaped vessel for incense produced in Athens in the fifth century B.C. It was discovered during excavations in the town of Phanagoria on the Northern Black Sea Coast.

The bronze cover from a funeral urn bearing the depiction of a feasting youth was created by an Etruscan master craftsman in the fourth century B.C. The Etruscans used to bury their noble people in tombs resembling stone palaces.

In the third century B.C. Ancient Rome came to the forefront of world history. In the field of art the Romans fell under a strong influence of ancient Greeks. The colossal marble statue of *Jupiter*, the main deity in the Roman pantheon, bears resemblance to the Greek god Zeus in appearance. Probably the anonymous first-century sculptor modelling this statue was inspired by the statue of *Zeus of Olympus* created by the great Phidias in the fifth century B.C.

The culmination of Roman fine arts was portraiture. The Hermitage possesses a fine collection of Roman sculptural portraits of the first century B.C. to fourth century A.D. Visitors seem to pass the history of Ancient Rome represented in personal images − from austere patricians of the Late Republic to the Roman Emperors captured in the state of spiritual depression, the time of the fall of the Empire.

380 ***Portrait of Antinoë.* 2nd century.**
Marble. Height 39.8 cm. Rome

381 **Torso of the statue of an emperor in armour.
First half of the 2nd century.** Marble. Height 155 cm. Rome

382
***Emperor Augustus as Jupiter.* 1st century**
Marble. Height 187 cm. Rome

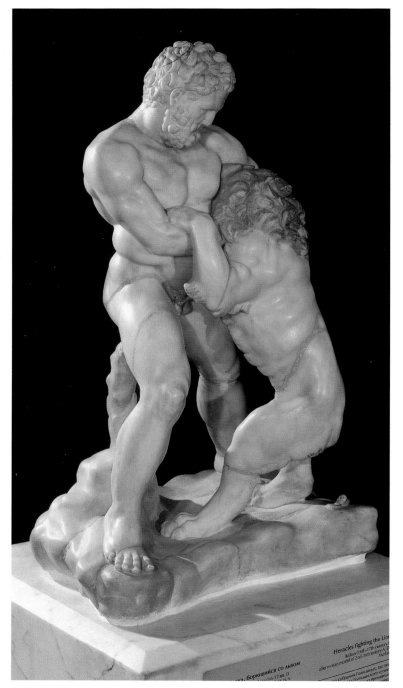

383
***Hercules Struggling with
the Lion* 2nd or 3rd century.
Rome. Additions: 17th century**
Italy. Marble. Height 63 cm

384 >
***Portrait of Cornelia Salonina,
Consort of Emperor Gallienus*
Mid-3rd century**
Marble. Height 57 cm. Rome

385 >
***Portrait of a Roman*
About mid-3rd century**
Marble. Rome

386 >
**Sarcophagus:
The History of Hippolytus.
Late 2nd century**
Marble. Height 125 cm. Rome

ITALY: 16TH TO 18TH CENTURY

Some masterpieces of Italian art of the sixteenth century and Italian art of the seventeenth and eighteenth century can be found in the halls and rooms of the New Hermitage. As is known, the core of the Hermitage's collection of Italian painting was formed in the last quarter of the eighteenth century, under Catherine the Great, and the most significant for the "Italian" section of the Empress's gallery were the Paris collection of Baron Pierre Crozat (1772) and that of Sir Robert Walpole (1779) at Houghton Hall in England. Michelangelo's sculpture *The Crouching Boy* entered the Hermitage with the collection of the Englishman John Lyde Browne (1785). The nineteenth century was marked by the acquisition of *Youth with a Lute* by Caravaggio and *The Conestabile Madonna* by Raphael.

After the revolution of 1917 the Italian collection of the Hermitage markedly increased owing to the transfer of some part of objects from the Museum of the Baron Stieglitz Central School of Technical Drawing. Unfortunately in the 1920s and 1930s, when the Soviet government sold works by the Old Masters to foreign art collectors, the Italian collection suffered an irreparable loss – the Hermitage lost a series of outstanding works, including canvases by Titian, Veronese and Raphael. At the present time works of Italian art come to the Hermitage mainly through the museum's Purchasing Committee.

The works of decorative art by Italian craftsmen of the fifteenth and sixteenth centuries are displayed in the Majolica Hall resembling an ancient basilica. The interior owes its name to varicoloured ceramic articles called *majolica* in Italy. Displayed in the Majolica Hall are also two paintings by Raphael, the greatest painter of the High Renaissance called "divine" even during his life. His *Holy Family* entered the Hermitage with the Crozat collection (1772), while *The Conestabile Madonna* was purchased in 1870 by orders of Alexander II for his consort Empress Maria Alexandrovna.

The large-scale paintings that in the sixteenth to eighteenth century had decorated cathedrals and palatial interiors, occupy the Large and Small Italian Skylight Halls. An indubitable masterpiece of late sixteenth-century painting is *The Birth of St John the Baptist* by Titian's pupil Jacopo Robusti, called Tintoretto, the last great Venetian of the Renaissance. This huge painting, resembling a magnificent carpet, is on display next to works by seventeenth-century masters. The Hermitage collection of seventeenth-century Italian painting is one of the best in Europe.

In 1585 the brothers Lodovico, Agostino and Annibale Carracci founded in Bologna the "Academy of those who took the right way". The adherents of Academicism strove to attain the "ideal beauty" implemented in works by the best artists of the High Renaissance and primarily Raphael. The founders of the Academy asserted that any individual ardour of the painter "should be restrained and any passion should be extinguished". The Bolognese Academic painters are represented in the Hermitage by works of Annibale Carracci, Domenichino and Guido Reni.

< 387
Raphael (Rafaello Santi)
(1483–1520). *The Holy Family*
(The Madonna with the Beardless St Joseph).
Ca **1506.** Tempera and oil on canvas,
transferred from a panel. 72.5 x 56.5 cm. Italy

388
Raphael (Rafaello Santi) (1483–1520)
The Madonna and Child
(The Conestabile Madonna). Ca **1503**
Tempera on canvas, transferred from a panel.
17.5 x 18 cm. Italy

241

Displayed in the so-called "Italian Cabinets" are small-scale canvases by Italian painters of the late sixteenth to eighteenth century. One can see here the only Hermitage's painting by Caravaggio (Michelangelo Merisi), acquired in 1808 from the Roman art collector Giustiniani. The great artist, who was the first to turn from the depiction of an ideal world to the depiction of common reality, is represented by his early work, *Youth with a Lute*, painted at the age of twenty-four years. The powerful, robust and somewhat "crude" style of Bernardo Strozzi echoes Caravaggio's painting.

Caravaggio's manner of painting marked by originality opposed the principles of the academic painters. The great French painter Nicolas Poussin would call him "a destroyer of painting". Nevertheless such adherents of Academicism as Massimo Stanzione, Carlo Dolci, Carlo Maratti and Luca Giordano would use many of Caravaggio's technical devices, especially his sharp contrasts of light and shade.

Towards the eighteenth century Italian art gradually lost its leading positions yielding the palm to French artists. The last to inherit the renown of the great Italian masters were representatives of the Venetian school of painting. Romantic urban landscapes, the so-called *vedutas*, painted with topographical precision by the famous Antonio Canale (Canaletto), were literally filled with space, air and light. On a par with the leading Italian artists was the outstanding decorative painter Giovanni Battista Tiepolo, whose sumptuous and grand style appeared as a powerful finale completing the long history of early Italian art.

< 389
Plate with a depiction of St Cecilia.
Between 1540 and 1545
Majolica, painted over white opaque glazing, lustre.
Diameter 41 cm. Deruta, Italy

< 390
Apothecary vessel. Early 16th century
Majolica, painted over white opaque glazing.
Height 40 cm. Italy

391
Apothecary jar.
Between 1505 and 1510
Majolica, painted over white
opaque glazing.
Height 26 cm. Deruta, Italy

392
Master Niccolo da Urbino.
Dish: *The Rape of Helen.*
***Ca* 1519.** Majolica, painted
over white opaque glazing.
Diameter 52 cm. Urbino, Italy

< 393
Giovanni Biliverti (1576–1644)
Tobias Parting with the Angel
First quarter of the 17th century
Oil on canvas. 188.5 x 144.5 cm. Italy

394
**Caravaggio (Michelangelo Merisi
da Caravaggio) (1571–1610).**
A Youth with a Lute. Ca **1595**
Oil on canvas. 94 x 119 cm. Italy

395
Bernardo Strozzi (1581–1644).
The Healing of Tobias. Ca **1635**
Oil on canvas. 158 x 223.5 cm. Italy

< 396
Carlo Dolci (1616–1686)
St Cecilia. Ca **1670**
Oil on canvas.
126 x 99.5 cm. Italy

< 397
**Carlo Maratti
(1625–1713)**
*Portrait of Pope
Clement IX.* **1660s**
Oil on canvas.
170 x 123 cm. Italy

< 398
**Tintoretto
(Jacopo Robusti)
(1518–1594)**
*The Birth of
St John the Baptist.
Ca* **1550.** Oil on canvas.
181 x 266 cm. Italy

399
**Massimo Stanzione
(1585–1656).** *Cleopatra*
1630s. Oil on canvas.
169 x 99.5 cm. Italy

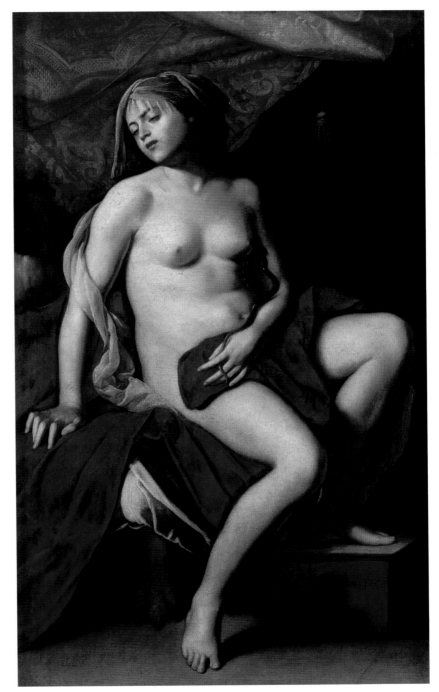

< 400
**Giovanni Baptista Tiepolo
(1696–70)**
*The Triumph of an Army
Commander. Ca* **1725**
Oil on canvas. 546 x 322 cm. Italy

401
**Antonio Canale
(Canaletto). (1697–1768)**
*Reception of the French
Ambassador in Venice.* **1726**
Oil on canvas. 181 x 259.5 cm. Italy

402
**Giovanni Baptista Tiepolo
(1696–70)**
*Maecenas Presenting the Liberal
Arts to Emperor Augustus. Ca* **1745**
Oil on canvas. 69.5 x 89 cm. Italy

Although the Hermitage collection of Spanish painting covering the period from the fifteenth to nineteenth century numbers about 150 canvases, it is one of the best and most representative Spanish collections outside Spain. For a long time European art collectors neglected Spanish painting, which was largely due to the relatively isolated character of artistic life in this major monarchy of the Old World. Only paintings by Velázquez, Ribera and especially Murillo were in high demand. The discovery of the specific character of Spanish culture by other European peoples took place merely at the beginning of the nineteenth century, in the period of Napoleonic Wars, when an immense number of treasures brought from Spain appeared at European sales. In 1814 Alexander I acquired a large collection of Spanish pictures from the English banker Coesevelt that made up the nucleus of the Hermitage collection of Spanish painting represented before merely by rare examples. In the nineteenth century the Hermitage acquired paintings of the Spanish masters from the collections of Joséphine de Beauharnais and the Spanish minister Manuel de Godoy. Some individual masterpieces were acquired at auctions. In 1911 Piotr Durnovo presented to the Hermitage a painting by El Greco. After the revolution of 1917 a number of fifteenth-century Spanish paintings entered the Hermitage and in 1972 the American art collector Armand Hammer presented to the Hermitage as a gift a canvas by the great Francisco Goya.

Although Spain is situated not far from Italy, Spanish culture and art developed in a different way of its own. In the eighth century the country was conquered by the Moslem Arabs and for seven centuries the Spaniards fought for their liberation. A constant sense of threat and readiness for self-sacrifice engendered such features of the national character as bravery, honesty, pride, ardour and magnanimity. The Christian Church that headed the Reconquista played a special role in Spanish life. A sincere piety and noble simplicity gave birth to the "solid and austere manner" of Spanish artists. The most popular kinds of painting in Spain were religious painting and portraiture.

Art of the fifteenth century connected with Gothic traditions is represented in the Hermitage by paintings that had once belonged to *retablos* – church altarpieces incorporating painting and sculpture. Sixteenth-century painting, created under the influence of Italian masters, is represented by paintings of the "divine" Luis Morales permeated with severe asceticism, the formal portraits from the age of Philip II, the time of the highest flowering of Spanish monarchy, and the masterpiece of the great El Greco (Domenikos Theotokopoulos) – *The Apostles Peter and Paul*.

The seventeenth century marked by the emergence of a whole galaxy of fine artists became the "Golden Age" of Spanish painting. The first Spanish artist to receive recognition in Italy was Hosé de

< 403
Paolo de San Leocadio (tondo) *St Joachim Meeting St Anne at the Golden Gate.* **Early 16th century**
Tempera and oil on panel. 167.5 x 88.5 cm. Spain

404
Unknown Spanish Artist of the Castilian School) *The Entombment.* **Second half of the 15th century**
Tempera and oil on panel. 94 x 182 cm. Spain

405
Juan Pantoja de la Cruz (1553–1608) *Portrait of Diego de la Villamayor.* **1605**
Oil on canvas. 89 x 71 cm. Spain

406
Luis de Morales (1520/25–1585) *The Madonna and Child with a Cross-Shaped Distaff*
Oil on canvas, transferred from a panel. 71.5 x 52 cm. Spain

Ribera, who was active in the residence of the Spanish Viceroy in Naples. A follower of Caravaggio, Ribera combined in his works the vigour of life of the great Italian painter with an inspired propagation of Christianity. His successor in Spain was Francisco de Zurbarán nicknamed the "Spanish Caravaggio". Highly pious like Ribera, Zurbarán, with all his epic monumentality, "seems to be a naïve and sincere child".

The greatest Spanish painter Diego Velázquez, "the most painterly among painters", is represented in the Hermitage by two canvases. His youthful picture *Luncheon*, already demonstrating his unrivalled mastery, depicts a merry scene in a tavern, called *bodegone* in Spain. The Hermitage's *Portrait of the Count-Duke of Olivares* is a work by the mature Velázquez, Court Painter to Philip IV. The portrait of the King's almighty favourite strikes us by its living force and merciless truth.

The last great Spanish artist of the golden century became Bartolomé Esteban Murillo, called the "Spanish Raphael" for his tender delicacy and lyricism.

In the eighteenth century Spanish painting, under the influence of foreign masters, lost its specific national features. Only at the end of the century there emerged Francisco Goya, a painter of genius, who evolved new paths in art. The Hermitage owns his *Portrait of the Actress Antonia Zárate* painted by the artist in the early nineteenth century.

407
Francisco de Zurbarán (1598–1664)
St Lawrence. **1636**
Oil on canvas. 292 x 225 cm. Spain

408
Francisco de Zurbarán (1598–1664)
The Girlhood of the Madonna. Ca **1660**
Oil on canvas. 73.5 x 53.5 cm. Spain

El Greco (Domenikos Theotokopoulos) (1541–1614)
The Apostles Peter and Paul. **Between 1587 and 1592.** Oil on canvas. 121.5 x 105 cm. Spain

410
Diego Velázquez (1599–1660)
Luncheon. Ca **1617–18.** Oil on canvas. 108 x 102 cm. Spain

411
**Francisco Hosé de Goya
y Lucientes (1746–1828)**
*Portrait of the Actress
Antonia Zárate.* **1810–11**
Oil on canvas.
71 x 58 cm. Spain

412
**Diego Velázquez
(1599–1660)**
*Portrait of the Count
Duke of Olivares.* **Ca 1640**
Oil on canvas.
67 x 54.5 cm. Spain

413
**Antonio de Pereda
(1608–1678).**
Still Life. **1652**
Oil on canvas.
80 x 94 cm. Spain

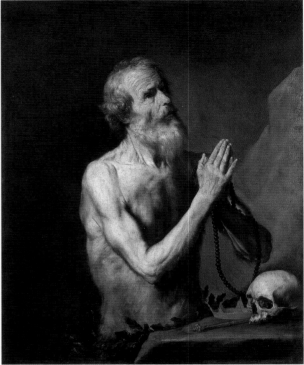

414
**Bartolomé Esteban Murillo
(1617–1682)** *Vision of St Anthony
of Padua.* **1675–80**
Oil on canvas. 130 x 104 cm. Spain

415
Hosé de Ribera (1591–1652)
St Onuphrius. **1637**
Oil on canvas. 130 x 104 cm. Spain

416
Hosé de Ribera (1591–1652)
St Sebastian and St Irene. **1628**
Oil on canvas. 156 x 188 cm. Spain

417 >
Hosé de Ribera (1591–1652)
*St Jerome Listening
to the Sound of a Trumpet.* **1626**
Oil on canvas. 185 x 133 cm. Spain

418
Bartolomé Esteban Murillo (1617–1682)
Rest on the Flight into Egypt.
Between 1665 and 1670
Oil on canvas. 136.5 x 179.5 cm. Spain

419
Bartolomé Esteban Murillo (1617–1682)
Boy with a Dog. **1650s**
Oil on canvas. 74 x 60 cm. Spain

420 >
Bartolomé Esteban Murillo (1617–1682)
The Immaculate Conception. **1670s**
Oil on canvas. 195.5 x 145 cm. Spain

HOLLAND: 16TH AND 17TH CENTURIES

The Hermitage collection of Dutch painting of the seventeenth and eighteenth centuries is one of the largest and best in Europe. The first pictures by Dutch artists acquired for Peter the Great came to St Petersburg as early as 1716. Masterpieces of Dutch painting entered the museum with all major collections acquired by Catherine the Great in the eighteenth century. Some excellent works came to the Hermitage with the Malmaison collection bought by Alexander I in the early nineteenth century. In 1915 the museum supplemented its stocks with a vast collection of the so-called "Small Dutchmen" of the Russian geographer Piotr Semionov-Tien-Shansky. It contained 719 paintings by 340 artists. Later the Dutch collection grew considerably due to private collections nationalized after the revolution. A number of masterpieces was bought by the Hermitage Purchasing Commission. The best works of the Dutch collection of seventeenth- and eighteenth-century painting are displayed in seven halls of the New Hermitage.

In 1609 seven northern Netherlandish provinces, after a long struggle against Spain, gained their independence and came to be called the Republic of the United Provinces or Holland. In that period three quarters of the Dutchmen lived in cities and towns and were engaged in free labour, mainly trade and sea-faring; severe Protestantism dominated their religious life. All that made its imprint upon art that was to cater the tastes of the industrious and free Dutch burgher, who liked comfort and well-done things.

The artist's profession ceased to be unique and paintings turned into a usual good, if highly demanded. The painters focused on common reality as their subject-matter and among their customers were merchants, burghers, craftsmen and even peasants. This lead to an increase in the number of artists specializing in different kinds of painting: landscape, still life or everyday scenes.

The period from the 1630s to 1680s saw the flowering of Dutch painting. Among a great deal of artistically inexpressive, but well executed paintings from this period there occur veritable masterpieces created by excellent artists. One cannot help amazing at the unbelievable virtuosity and seeming ease of handling characteristic of portraits by the great Frans Hals. His work was "a brilliant rapid copying of the real world". Having numerous pupils, Hals did not left followers – his manner of painting proved to be inimitable. Jan van Goyen, a creator of the intimate panoramic landscape, painted charming views of his native Holland. Pictures by Jacob van Ruisdael, of whom Goethe said that "this thinking artist revealing himself as a poet attains consummate symbolism", are pervaded with a profound philosophical interpretation of nature.

Especially popular with Dutch artists were paintings of everyday subjects divided into two trends – genre scenes from the life of high society and depictions of common people. The first trend is represented in the Hermitage by famous works of the exquisite Gabriel Metsu, the somewhat mannered

< 421 **Rembrandt Harmensz van Rijn**
(1606–1669) *The Holy Family.* **1645.**
Oil on canvas. 117 x 91 cm. Holland

422 **Rembrandt Harmensz van Rijn**
(1606–1669) *Flora.* **1634.**
Oil on canvas. 125 x 101 cm. Holland

423 Rembrandt Harmensz van Rijn (1606–1669). *The Sacrifice of Abraham.* **1635**
Oil on canvas. 193 x 132 cm. Holland

lyrical artist Frans van Mieris, the master of interior painting Pieter de Hooch and the brilliant Gerard Terborch. The foremost artist of the second trend was the mischievous Adriaen van Ostade and his pupil, Jan Steen, "the most real painter of people", who painted scenes from the life of both burghers and peasants tinged with humour.

A place apart in Dutch painting belongs to Paulus Potter, simultaneously a subtle landscape artist and a fine animal painter. Dutch masters of still life painting demonstrate an amazing mastery in the depiction of gifts of nature and creations of human hands.

But all that vivid, noisy and talented community of artists remains in the background of the brilliant Rembrandt Harmensz van Rijn, a solitary genius denying any definitions or classifications. The artist who was born and spent his whole life in Holland, from the very beginning of his independent career revealed himself as a creator of universal significance. His tragic destiny, according to Alexander Benois, was "a veritable Calvary, an ordeal unbearable for average people." The Hermitage owns more than twenty canvases by Rembrandt illustrating all periods of his creative biography. From his earlier works shining with great happiness and joy of living to the last ones when the artist's soul began to "cry with bloody tears". Rembrandt is the only painter of Holland who was equally successful in diverse genres. He excelled in his portraits revealing the depths of human soul and in elaborate large-scale canvases permeated with tormenting philosophical thoughts, the pride of place among which goes to the majestic *Return of the Prodigal Son* painted by Rembrandt shortly before his death.

424 **Rembrandt Harmensz van Rijn (1606–1669)**
***Young Woman Trying Earrings.* 1657**
Oil on canvas. 39.5 x 32.5 cm. Holland

425 **Rembrandt Harmensz van Rijn (1606–1669)**
***David and Jonathan.* 1642**
Oil on panel. 73 x 61.5 cm. Holland

426
Rembrandt Harmensz van Rijn (1606–1669)
Danaë. **1636–42.**
Oil on canvas. 185 x 202.5 cm. Holland

427 >
Rembrandt Harmensz van Rijn (1606–1669)
Descent from the Cross. **1634**
Oil on canvas. 158 x 117 cm. Holland

428
Rembrandt Harmensz van Rijn (1606–1669)
David and Uriah. Ca **1665**
Oil on canvas. 125 x 116 cm. Holland

429 >
Rembrandt Harmensz van Rijn (1606–1669)
The Return of the Prodigal Son. **1668–69**
Oil on canvas. 262 x 205 cm. Holland

430
Paulus Potter (1625–1654)
Punishment of a Hunter.
Ca **1647.** Oil on panel.
84.5 x 120 cm. Holland

431
Jost Cornelisz
Droochsloot (1586–1666)
Winter in a Dutch Town
Oil on panel. 50.5 x 74.5 cm.
Holland

432
**Jacob van Ruisdael
(1628/29–1682)**
The Marsh. **1660s.** Oil on canvas.
72.5 x 99 cm. Holland

433
Paulus Potter (1625–1654)
Farm. **1649.** Oil on panel.
81 x 115.5 cm. Holland

434
Adriaen van Ostade
(1610–1685)
The Sense of Eyesight. **1635.**
From the series *Five Senses*
Oil on panel. 20 x 25 cm. Holland

435
Adriaen van Ostade
(1610–1685)
The Sense of Taste. **1635.**
From the series *Five Senses*
Oil on panel. 20 x 25 cm. Holland

436
Frans Hals
(1581 – between 1585 and 1666)
Portrait of a Young Man
Holding a Glove. Ca **1650.**
Oil on canvas.
80 x 66.5 cm. Holland

437 >
Jan Steen (1625/26–1679)
The Revellers. Ca **1660**
Oil on panel. 39 x 30 cm. Holland

438
**Willem Claesz Heda
(1594 – between
1680 and 1682)**
Breakfast with a Lobster.
1648. Oil on canvas.
118 x 118 cm. Holland

439
**Balthasar van der Ast
(1593/94–1657)**
Still Life with Fruit.
1620s. Oil on panel.
75 x 104 cm. Holland

440 >
**Gerard Ter Borch
(1617–1681)**
The Glass of Lemonade.
1660s. Oil on canvas,
transferred from a panel.
67 x 54 cm. Holland

441 >
**Peter de Hooch
(1629 – after 1684)**
A Woman and Her Maid.
Ca **1660.** Oil on canvas.
53 x 42 cm. Holland

442 >
**Frans Jansz
van Mieris the Elder
(1635–1681)**
Morning of a Young Lady.
Ca **1659–60.** Oil on panel.
51.5 x 39.5 cm. Holland

443 >
Gabriel Metsu (1629–1667)
*A Sick Woman and
Her Doctor.* **1660s**
Oil on canvas.
61.5 x 47.5 cm. Holland

444
Gerard Dou (1613–1675)
Old Woman Reading.
Ca **1660–65.** Oil on panel.
32 x 23 cm. Holland

445
Gerard Dou (1613–1675)
Old Woman Unwinding a
Thread Roll. Ca **1660–65**
Oil on panel. 32 x 23 cm. Holland

446
Adriaen van Ostade
(1610–1685)
The Sense of Hearing. **1635**
From the series *Five Senses*
Oil on panel. 20 x 25 cm. Holland

447
**Pieter Cornelisz van Slingeland
(1640–1691)**
Breakfast of a Young Man
Second half of the 17th century
Oil on canvas. 22 x 18.5 cm. Holland

448
**Frans Jansz van
Mieris the Younger (1689–63)**
Peasant Man with a Jug. **1731**
Oil on panel. 17 x 13.5 cm. Holland

449
Jan van Goyen (1596–1656)
Boats on the Bank of a River. Ca 1648
Oil on panel. Diameter 15.5 cm. Holland

FLANDERS: 17TH AND 18TH CENTURIES

The Hermitage possesses one of the best collections of seventeenth-century Flemish painting, the specific feature of which is a large number of works by leading artists of Flanders – Pieter Paul Rubens, Anthonis van Dyck, Frans Snyders and Jacob Jordaens. Most of these paintings came to the museum under Catherine the Great, when works of Flemish artists were widely popular with art lovers and occupied a place of honour in all major collections. The most important addition to the Flemish collection in the nineteenth century became paintings from the Malmaison collection (1814) and in the twentieth century the paintings from the collection of Piotr Semionov-Tien-Shansky (1915). A number of masterpieces of Flemish painting were transferred to the Hermitage after the revolution of 1917 from nationalized private collections. Today the Hermitage collection of Flemish painting numbers over 500 paintings. Their best part is displayed in five rooms of the New Hermitage.

In the first half of the seventeenth century Flanders – the southern part of the Netherlands that remained under the power of the Spanish kings after the Netherlandish revolution of the sixteenth century – saw an unusual flowering of the fine arts and especially of painting. There emerged a whole galaxy of excellent painters, each of whom could glorify any European state. The specific feature of Flemish painting of the period was its monolithic character, which can be accounted for by the presence among the artists of an outstanding leader – Pieter Paul Rubens, the creator of a unique style who exerted a great influence on the development of Western European art. Rubens placed over his house an ancient Roman saying reading: *Spiritus sanctus in corpore sancti* ("A sound mind in a sound body") that exactly reflected the life position of this "god of painters" revealed in his intense, dynamic and life-asserting painting. The creative scope of Rubens was truly immense: from monumental canvases to intimate portraits and lyrical landscapes. The Hermitage collection numbering nearly forty paintings by the Flemish painter of genius cover nearly the whole range of his work.

Rubens was the creator of a famous workshop where nearly all major Flemish artists improved their skills. The most outstanding among them was Anthonis van Dyck, who won recognition as an independent master and was accepted to the Guild of St Luke as early as at the age of 18. Van Dyck devoted most of his efforts to portraiture. He could render as nobody else in the glance of a sitter the intensity of his or her intense inner life and the subtlest nuances of feelings. Soon the popularity of Van Dyck went beyond the borders of Flanders and he began to work in different countries. In 1632 the artist was invited by the English King Charles I and to the end of his days remained his court painter. In England Van Dyck

created portraits of representatives of high society, which personified the ideal of English aristocracy and became models of imitation for burgeoning English painting.

Frans Snyders, a major master of still-life painting, also worked in Rubens's workshop. Imbibing the heroic pathos of his great teacher, Snyders created a new type of monumental still life, depicting with an amazing force and precision not only the "dead nature", but living creatures, too. It was not for nothing that contemporaries called Snyders's paintings just "shops".

The fame of the "most Flemish" painter belongs to Jacob Jordaens, whose art, scintillating with invigorating merriment, is inseparable from traditional Netherlandish painting. Infatuated with Rubens's ideas, he retained his own, more earthly perception of things. He is in his element in the atmosphere of a folk festival permeated with humour and revealing the best features of the Flemish character – open-hearted friendliness and the boundless joy of living.

Jan Brueghel, the creator of "intimate" landscapes intended for smaller interiors, also worked in the studio of Rubens. He was nicknamed the "Velvet Brueghel" at first for his love of velvet and later for a soft, velvet-like tonality of his paintings.

A place apart in Flemish painting belongs to Adriaen Brower, a "painter of comic genre scenes", who had a keen insight into the somewhat crude everyday life of common Flemish people and sometimes tinged his works with irony.

The painting of David Teniers the Younger reflects the pastoral moods of the second half of the seventeenth century that ousted the heroic pathos of Rubens's golden century.

< 450
Pieter Paul Rubens (1577–1640)
Descent from the Cross. Ca 1617 – 1618
Oil on canvas. 297 x 200 cm. Flanders

451
Pieter Paul Rubens (1577–1640)
Perseus and Andromeda. Early 1620s. Oil on canvas, transferred from a panel. 99.5 x 139 cm. Flanders

452 **Pieter Paul Rubens (1577–1640)**
Feast at the House of
Simon the Pharisee
Between1618 and 1620
(with his pupils). Oil on canvas,
transferred from a panel.
189 x 254.5 cm. Flanders

453 **Pieter Paul Rubens (1577–1640)**
The Roman Charity (Cimon and Pero)
Ca **1612.** Oil on canvas, transferred
from a panel. 140.5 x 180.3 cm. Flanders

454 > **Pieter Paul Rubens (1577–1640)**
The Union of Earth and Water. Ca **1618**
Oil on canvas. 222.5 x 180.5 cm. Flanders

279

< 455 **Anthonis van Dyck (1599–1641).**
Family Portrait (The Family of the Landscape
Painter Jan Wildens?). **Late 1621**
Oil on canvas. 113.5 x 93.5 cm. Flanders

456 **Anthonis van Dyck (1599–1641).**
Self-Portrait. **Late 1620s – early 1630s.**
Oil on canvas. 116.5 x 93.5 cm. Flanders

457 **Anthonis van Dyck (1599–1641).** *Portrait of Sir*
Thomas Wharton. **Second half of the 1630s.**
Oil on canvas. 217 x 128.5 cm. Flanders

458 **Anthonis van Dyck (1599–1641)**
Portrait of Philadelphia and Elizabeth Wharton
Second half of the 1630s. Oil on canvas.
162 x 130 cm. Flanders

< 459 **Frans Snyders (1579–1657)**
Vegetable Shop. **Between
1618 and 1621.** Oil on canvas.
208 x 341 cm. Flanders

< 460 **Frans Snyders (1579–1657)**
Fruit Shop. **Between
1618 and 1621.** Oil on canvas.
206 x 342 cm. Flanders

461 **Jacob Jordaens (1593–1678)**
The Bean King. Ca **1638.** Oil on
canvas. 157 x 211 cm. Flanders

462 **Jan Fyt (1611–1661)**
Fruit and Parrot. **1645**
Oil on canvas, transferred from
a panel. 58.3 x 90.7 cm. Flanders

**David Teniers the Younger
(1610–1690)
A Peasant Wedding. 1650**
Oil on canvas.
82 x 108 cm. Flanders

463

464

**Adraien Brouwer (1605–1638)
*Scene in a Tavern
(A Rural Violinist).* 1634–38**
Oil on panel.
25 x 33.5 cm. Flanders

465
**Jan Brueghel the Elder
(the Velvet Brueghel)
(1568–1625).**
A Country Road. **Between
1608 and 1610.** Oil on panel.
48 x 67 cm. Flanders

466
**Jan Brueghel the Elder
(the Velvet Brueghel)
(1568–1625).** *The Edge of
a Forest (Flight into Egypt)*
1610. Oil on copper plate.
25 x 36 cm. Flanders

THE TREASURE GALLERY

The Hermitage's collection of jewellery amounts to several thousand articles of gold, silver and precious stones created in different ages by masters from various countries. Its best part was displayed in the specially equipped interiors – the Treasure Gallery-1 (Diamond Room) in the New Hermitage and the Treasure Gallery- 2 (Gold Room) in the Winter Palace. The display consists of two large sections.

The archaeological part of the collection is formed of valuable finds from ancient burial tombs. The earliest examples of the jeweller's art kept in the Hermitage are artifacts dating to the fourth and third millennia B.C. from the Maikop burial mound discovered at the end of the nineteenth century in the Northern Caucasus. World-famous are the jewellery objects of the seventh century B.C. to the first century A.D. yielded by burials of the chieftains of nomadic tribes. The ancient Scythian barrows, where digging began as early as the reign of Catherine the Great, yielded superb objects produced of gold and silver in the "beast style" characteristic of the nomads' art. The acknowledged masterpiece of the collection is a silver amphora for wine of the fourth century B.C. from the Chertomlyk burial mound, a work by an unknown ancient Greek master craftsman.

The second section contains jewelled objects from the Middle Ages to the early twentieth century. A unique memorial of medieval art is a sil-

ver reliquary shaped like the figure of a deacon made in the twelfth century in France and acquired for the Hermitage as part of the collection of Alexander Basilewsky in 1885. The majority of the works of Russian church art of the sixteenth to the early twentieth century, created mainly in the workshops of Moscow, entered the museum after the revolution of 1917 from the cathedral of the Winter Palace. Gold and silver crosses, icon mounts, liturgical vessels and priests' vestments lavishly embellished with gemstones and pearls were especially favoured in Russia.

The nucleus of the second section consists of the jewellery that belonged to the Russian Empresses Anna Ioannovna, Elizabeth Petrovna and Catherine the Great. The latter allotted for her jewellery a special "diamond" room, where innumerable quantity of precious objects, sometimes used as presentation pieces, were kept in special cabinets. In 1792 the jewellery was transferred from the Winter Palace to the block of the Raphael Loggias and from the middle of the nineteenth century the Treasure Gallery occupied one of the galleries of the Small Hermitage. The state regalia – the crown, the scepter and the orb of the Russian monarchs – were also preserved there. In 1914, in connection with a threat of the front approaching to Petrograd, the regalia were transferred to Moscow and nowadays they can be found in the Diamond Fund of Russia there. The Hermitage owns a fine scale model of the re-

< 467 **Bullock. 4th–3rd millennium B.C.**
Gold. 7.6 x 6 cm. Maikop burial mound, Northern Caucasus

468 **Reliquary in the form of a deacon:** *St Stephen.* **Late 12th century.** Gold, silver, gems and wood. Height 42.5 cm. France

469 **Vessel with representations. 4th–3rd millennium B.C.**
Silver. Height 9.6 cm. Maikop burial mound, Northern Caucasus

470 **Amphora. 4th century B.C.** Silver-gilt.
Height 70 cm. Chertomlyk burial mound, Dnieper area

471
Second half of the 18th century. Craftsman: Yakov Frolov (mount: 1775)
Tempera on panel. Silver-gilt, pearls, gemstones and glass. 33.1 x 28.6 cm. Russia

galia produced by jewellers of the famous Fabergé Company in 1900.

The display offers a wide variety of silver and golden goblets, vessels of rock crystal in mounts of noble metals, presentation dishes and saltcellars, table clocks with musical mechanisms and of course a superb collection of jewellery.

A passion for precious decorative objects accompanied mankind since time immemorial and, notably, not only women liked to adorn their bodies, clothes, shoes and head-dresses. The favourite and fashionable detail of man's wear in the age of great geographic discoveries was a golden pendant with a "Baroque" pearl of whimsical shape. European aristocrats made it a precious addition to their costumes – set with diamonds, emeralds, sapphires and rubies, watches on chatelaines with small keys and a seal were worn on the belt in the middle and second half of the eighteenth century. The bodices and corsages of noble ladies' formal dresses were embellished with whole mineralogical collections set as shining and iridescent bouquets. Pockets and handbags of members of the richest families were embellished with precious knick-knacks; fine necessaires, perfume flasks of diverse shapes and last but not least – snuffboxes.

472
Diskos. 1670s. Gold, gemstones and enamel. Height 10 cm; Diameter 27 cm. Russia

473
Mitre. 1840s. Brocade, gold, silver, gemstones, pearls and silk. Height 22.5 cm. Russia

< 474 **Paperweight with the sculptural group** *St George.* **1830s–1840s**
Incised, chased and polished gold, silver, pearls, heliotrope, rubies and opals. Height 13.9 cm

< 475 **Mug. 1736–40.** Craftsman: Gottfried Wendt. Silver-gilt and emeralds. Height 24.5 cm. Poland

< 476 **Salt-cellar. 1797.**
Craftsman: Ivan Krag.
Gold, silver, diamonds and enamel. Height 20.6 cm. Russia

477 **Dagger and sheath. Mid-18th century**
Craftsman: Tak. Gold, steel, diamonds, rubies, emeralds, rock crystal and enamel. Length 43 cm. Iran

478 **Table clock with a toilet-case and musical mechanism. 1772**
Clock-maker: James Cox. Gold, silver, agate, pearls, glass and steel. Height 36.9 cm. England

479 **Peacock-shaped flask. 1780s**
Gold, silver, diamonds, enamel. 7.5 x 8.5 cm. Russia

480 **The Fabergé Company. The Imperial Regalia (scale model). 1900.** Gold, silver, diamonds, gemstones, pearls, velvet, rhodonite and wood.
The Large Crown: height 7.3 cm; diameter 5.4 cm.
The Small Crown: height 3.8 cm; diameter 2.9 cm.
Orb: height 3.8 cm; scepter: height 15.8 cm. Russia

< 481 Watch on a chatelaine. 1770s.
Gold, silver, diamonds, brilliants, glass and enamel.
Diameter 4.2 cm; length of the chatelaine 13 cm. Russia

482 **Bouquet of flowers. 1740s.** Jeweller: Jérémie Pauzié. Gold, silver,
precious and semi-precious stones, glass and fabric. 13 x 19 cm. Russia

483 **Pendant: *Swan. Ca* 1590.** Gold, gemstones, pearls and enamel.
9.2 x 5.9 cm. Netherlands

484 **Snuffbox: *Lisette.* 1780s.** By Johann Gottlieb Scharf.
Gold, silver, diamonds, brilliants, emeralds and enamel. Russia

THE MENSHIKOV PALACE

In 1981 the Hermitage opened its new exhibition, "Russian Culture of the First Three decades of the Eighteenth Century" at the University Embankment on Vasilyevsky Island, in one of few buildings of Peter's age that have reached us – in the palace of Alexander Menshikov, the first Governor of St Petersburg.

In 1703 Peter the Great presented the vast Vasilyevsky Island to his closest associate Prince Alexander Menshikov, the first Chief Commander of the Peter and Paul Fortress and Governor General of Ingermanland. A year later the prince ordered to lay out a garden and to build "wooden chambers" on the island.

The construction of the Stone Palace began in 1710, but it was being built, extended and redesigned during the subsequent fifteen years. Menshikov employed the best foreign architects engaged in the construction of the new city on the Neva, including Dominico Trezzini, Giovanni Mario Fontana, Johann Gottfried Schädel, Georg Johann Mattarnovy, Andreas Schlüter and Bartolomeo Carlo Rastrelli.

The palace was designed as a whole complex of buildings with dwelling apartments, state rooms and service blocks. All of them were linked with the central part of the palace by a roundabout gallery. On the Neva side the four-storeyed building with two side projections under a tall gabled roof was decorated by a portico with columns over a high porch and a portal with the prince's coat of arms. The pediments of the side projections were topped with vases and the prince's gilded crowns. A fenced landing-stage was arranged in front of the palace. Behind the main courtyard there stretched a beautiful garden with ponds and hothouses that produced a high yield of berries, fruit and vegetables.

Alexander Menshikov settled in the palace, called "the vastest and most beautiful in entire St Petersburg", in 1711. Peter the Great used to visit this luxurious and hospitable house; it was often the setting for receptions of foreign envoys, assemblies and masked balls. Events of state importance and festive dates of the royal family were celebrated in the palace. The palace witnessed its owner's breathtaking career to the utmost height of success and his no less swift fall. In 1727 the "Most Illustrious King of the Holy Roman Empire of the German Nation", Admiral and Generalissimo Alexander Menshikov was arrested, deprived of all positions and exiled together with his family to the remote Siberian town of Beriozov. There he buried his consort Darya Mikhailovna and their daughter Maria and died himself in 1729. Empress Anna Ioannovna brought Menshikov's son and daughter, who remained alive, back from their exile.

Originally the palace housed the chancelleries of some *collegia* or ministries and from 1732 it housed the Cadet Corps. Until the 1930s the Menshikov Palace was occupied by various military educational establishments. During the siege of Leningrad the mansion was used as a military hospital and after the war its rooms were converted into university lecture-halls. In 1966 the palace was handed over to

the Hermitage and specialists of the museum could start work on returning to the building of its original appearance. Despite significant alterations, a whole number of unique interior of the Menshikov Palace has been restored.

Like three centuries ago, present-day visitors pass through a huge vestibule with marble statues, enjoy works of fine and applied art collected by the prince and then ascend the oak staircase arranged to the entire height of the palace in the rooms of the first floor. Originally it had been the Great Hall here with two tiers of windows, huge mirrors, "unusually long, wide and tall", as foreign travellers stated (later the hall was redesigned into the church of the Cadet Corps). Worthy of special attention among the first-floor interiors are the rooms, the walls and ceilings of which are faced with Delft tiles painted in cobalt blue. Truly unique is the so-called Walnut Study of Alexander Menshikov, the interior of which was designed according to recommendations of the architect to the French Crown Jean-Baptiste Alexandre Le Blond as early as 1717.

< 488
The Antechamber (Foyer)

489
The Walnut Room (Walnut Study)

THE GENERAL STAFF BUILDING

In the early 1990s the State Hermitage came into possession of the eastern wing of the General Staff building put up by the outstanding architect Carlo Rossi in the first decades of the nineteenth century. This famous structure, one of the longest in the city, became a befitting completion to the famous complex of Palace Square. The central section of the General Staff facing the Winter Palace is emphasized by a majestic triumphal arch erected with a participation of the sculptors Stepan Pimenov and Vasily Demuth-Malinovsky in honour of the victory of the Russian arms in the War of 1812.

The western wing of the building was intended for the General Staff and other military establishments, while the eastern wing was to house the service rooms for officials of the ministries. The rooms and halls of the first floor of the eastern wing were occupied by the Minister of Foreign Affairs. The earliest owners of these apartments were Count Karl Robert Nesselrohde and Prince Alexander Gorchakov. The design of the first-floor rooms has practically remained unchanged, although during the years of Soviet power the General Staff building often changed its owners – from representatives of the "punitive bodies of the revolution" (the All-Russian Extraordinary Commission for the Suppression of Counter-Revolution) to research and medical establishments.

The first Hermitage's display opened in the ten restored halls of the former apartment of Chancellor Karl Nesselrohde was the exhibition "Under the Aegis of the Eagle: Art of the Empire". The Empire style, born in Napoleon's France, spread beyond its geographical borders in many countries of the world, being especially interesting and unusual in the artistic life of the Russian Empire. One of characteristic elements of décor in Empire-style applied art is the depiction of the eagle – the traditional symbolic element of the state emblem of major European countries – France, Germany, Austria-Hungary and Russia. The exhibition "Under the Aegis of the Eagle: Art of the Empire" acquaints visitors with fine examples of painting, graphic art, sculpture, numismatics and works of decorative and applied art executed by masters from different European countries in the first three decades of the nineteenth century. Especially impressive in the interiors designed by Carlo Rossi are the contemporary items of furniture made from the architect's own drawings as well as the mantel clock and gilded table decorations produced by the outstanding French bronzer Pierre Philippe Thomire.

In 2003 in the General Staff building was opened the Museum of the Guards that illustrates

490 **Arch of the General Staff. 1819–29**
Architect: Carlo Rossi; sculptors;
Stepan Pimenov, Vasily Demuth-Malinovsky

491 > **Pierre Bonnard (1867–1947). *Morning in Paris.*** **1911.** Oil on canvas. 76.5 x 121 cm. France

492 > **Pierre Bonnard (1867–1947). *Evening in Paris.*** **1911.** Oil on canvas. 76.5 x 121 cm. France

the history of the best part of the Russian army – from the emergence of the Guards in the early eighteenth century to their losses in the fields of the First World War.

A wide public response had the opening of the exhibition "Pierre Bonnard and Maurice Denis: Decorative Ensembles in the Collection of the Hermitage" arranged in the halls of the General Staff building. In 1907 the Moscow art collector Ivan Morozov commissioned from the French artist Maurice Denis a series of decorative panels *The Story of Psyche* for the decoration of the Concert Hall in his mansion. Several years later another French master, Pierre Bonnard, received Morozov's commission for a large triptych, *At the Mediterranean: The Panel Between the Columns* for the decoration of the main staircase. These monumental works entered the Hermitage with other paintings by French artists in 1948 from the then closed Moscow's Museum of New Western Art, but the Hermitage had no possibility to display them owing to their large dimensions. Nowadays the decorative panels and easel works by Maurice Denis and Pierre Bonnard together with works by other French painters of the late nineteenth and early twentieth century have found a befitting place in the exhibition rooms of the General Staff building.

493 **The Dining Room. 1819–27**
Architect: Carlo Rossi

494 **Mantel clock: *Cupid and Psyche.*
1799.** Workshop of Pierre
Philippe Thomire. Wood, marble,
gilded bronze. Height 61 cm. France

495 > **The Second Drawing Room.
Furniture in the Empire style.
From a drawing
by Carlo Rossi. 1817–18**
Workshop of Ivan Baumann, Russia

496 >> **View of Palace Square. Mutual action of the Hermitage Museum and the Hermitage Bridge Studio devoted to the 60th Anniversary of the Lifting of the Siege of Leningrad (2004)**